The Genius of Play

Celebrating the Spirit
of Childhood

Sally Jenkinson

Hawthorn Press

The Genius of Play © Copyright 2001 Sally Jenkinson

Sally Jenkinson is hereby identified as author of this work in accordance with Section 77 of the Copyright, Designs and Patent Act, 1988. She asserts and gives notice of her moral right under this Act.

Published by Hawthorn Press, Hawthorn House, 1 Lansdown Lane, Stroud, Gloucestershire, GL5 1BJ, UK
Tel: (01453) 757040 Fax: (01453) 751138
info@hawthornpress.com
www.hawthornpress.com

Cover illustration, extract from 'Kinderspiele', by Pieter Breugel
Cover design by Hawthorn Press
Typesetting by Hawthorn Press, Stroud, Glos.
Printed in the UK by The Bath Press, Bath

Grateful acknowledgment to:
The Kunsthistorisches Museum, Vienna, Austria, for 'Kinderspiele' by Pieter Breugel.
The Open University Press for colour photograph of boys playing with wood.
Harper's Weekly 11 Oct 1873, Massachusetts Historical Society for 'Shipbuilding, Gloucester Harbour' by Winslow Homer. The Winterthur Library: Printed Book and Periodical Collection for the drawing from 'Children's Delight: Bright Stories for Boys and Girls', Boston, 1889. Emma Aylett for her photographs of the Steiner Waldorf Kindergarten, North London.

Every effort has been made to trace the ownership of all copyrighted material. If any omission has been made, please bring this to the publisher's attention so that proper acknowledgment may be given in future editions.

British Library Cataloguing in Publication Data applied for

ISBN 1 903458 04 8

genius: attendant, tutelary spirit etc.

Oxford English Dictionary

Article 31 of The Convention on the Rights of the Child (adopted by the General Assembly of the United Nations, November 20, 1989). states:

1. Parties recognise the right of the child to rest and leisure, to engage in play and recreational activities appropriate to the age of the child and to participate freely in cultural life and the arts.

2. Parties shall respect and promote the right of the child to participate fully in cultural and artistic life and shall encourage the provision of appropriate and equal opportunities for cultural, artistic, recreational and leisure activity.

The Genius of Play is a well-researched book that makes a valuable contribution to the worldwide debate about childhood. Play lies at the heart of childhood and this book deepens our understanding and appreciation of the crucial benefits of play. Herein lie the roots of our capacity to act socially, exercise our imaginations, develop emotional literacy and face new intellectual challenges. The author also shows how play deprivation, from which many of our children suffer now, is a threat to our well being. For all those who are seriously concerned about our children this is essential reading.

Christopher Clouder, Alliance for Childhood

Sally has a genius for perceiving the essence of childhood. Her examples of children at play are charming but also profound, for they show us the depths of play and the tremendous significance of play in human life. She balances anecdotes with the insights of major educators, psychologists and child advocates revealing a rich world of literature and organizations devoted to the importance of children's play. In a time when childhood is endangered and play is a dying art this book serves children well and offers much help to adults struggling to understand the power of play.

Joan Almon

This is a book which many who work with play will find useful and challenging. Sally Jenkinson forays into play 'times past' and in so doing raises concerns about play 'times present'. The recollections of play provide an important historical lens through which to reflect upon opportunities and accomplishments of children's play today. Sally's deep commitment to the integrity of play will also provide fuel to the debate about 21st century 'technologically prescribed' play as an inhibitor of children's freedom to construct the world for themselves.

The Genius of Play encourages educators to attend to children's intentions as they watch them play, to try to understand what it is that children are working out. It encourages us to allow the spirit of play to come through in the way we provide space (in all its dimensions) for children to play with freedom.

This is an important addition to the growing collection of books which address the theme of play today. Sally Jenkinson encourages us to attend to play in the whole of children's lives, as well as in their early preschool and school experiences. It deserves to be widely read and will generate lively debate amongst early childhood educators.

Dr. Cathy Nutbrown
The University of Sheffield, School of Education

Contents

Thanks

Thanks to the three children of the past, Lesley Gray, John Arnold and Brian Agg, who will recognise themselves in the following chapters, and to all the other children whose words, deeds and images live between the covers of this book.

Thanks to all my colleagues and friends and to my husband Angus and my three children, Derwin, Hamish and Emily.

Foreword

by Mary Jane Drummond

What kind of a book is this? An invitation to remember one's own childhood and play; a scholarly and multi-disciplinary review of relevant research; a powerful argument for the significance of play in human development; a treasury of attentive observations of children's play, past and present; a passport to the realm of the subjunctive, where might and could, perhaps and 'what if?' take precedence over the present indicative; a survival guide for the adult who is committed to the cause of childhood; a set of unforgettable snapshots of children's lives – *The Genius of Play* takes all these parts, and more, many more.

Sally Jenkinson makes an early move in establishing the grand theme of the book; in her opening pages she introduces the reader to the metaphor of *journey* as a way of understanding what it is that children do, in their passage through time, from the here-and-now immediacy of their play with dens, dolls and dressing up clothes, on the way to their undefined and unpredictable futures. But it is not a simple route map that she offers; this book is in no sense a set of directions for swiftly moving from A to B, from young to old, from little to big, from incapable to competent, from illiterate to literate, from child to adult. There are multiple pathways through the world of children's play: the chapter headings indicate some of the important milestones that readers will pass as they trace the footsteps of the child, of all children, who are uncomplicatedly committed to their journey, without knowing in the least where it will lead them. It is Sally Jenkinson's particular talent that she never loses sight of the complexities of play; she trounces the benevolent educator's attempt to kidnap the spontaneity of play for a pre-specified learning objective, and spurns the triviality of what she categories as 'wrap-around play,' a contemptuous phrase for the kind of play that is shaped and defined by official directives.

From a mainstream educator's perspective, this book is a most welcome and long overdue antidote to the many recent publications that attempt to justify the place of children's play in educational settings in terms of early academic success. Sally Jenkinson presents a multi-dimensional rationale: she delineates the moral purposes of play, invoking the child's 'moral imagination', another telling phrase. She demonstrates both the emotional and social value of play, the child's work in the domains of empathy and solidarity; she documents the creativity and aesthetic of play. She generously illustrates the interpenetration of play and spoken language, in all its forms; she gives proper prominence to children as symbolists and surrealists, using the materials of the workaday world to represent the extraordinary conceptions of their imagination.

The expert witnesses she summons to defend her case are as multivarious as her arguments; her educational authorities include Erich Fromm, Kieran Egan, Margaret Lowenfeld, Tina Bruce, Janusz Korczak, Bruno Bettelheim, Vivien Gussin Paley, Iona and Peter Opie. But there are other more divergent voices willing to testify in the cause of children's play, and Sally Jenkinson skilfully weaves their thoughts into her text, to sustain and enrich her advocacy; the reader will meet George Eliot, John Keats, Einstein, Coleridge, R. L. Stevenson and Rainer Maria Rilke.

This multiplicity of authority, reference point and argument is reflected in the illustrative examples of children's play that stud the pages of this book, like cloves in a sweet-smelling orange. Very few hundred words go by without a vivid glimpse of a real child, doing real play, from the reckless charioteer, steering an old pram chassis, whom we meet on the very first page, to the child with an illicit and covetous passion for the stone angels in a nearby cemetery. Here is a five year old creating an island of peace and absorption in a busy kindergarten as she breast-feeds her doll; here are some lucky children playing in the frothy white seclusion of a den created by suspending a lacy wedding dress between a washing line and a leafy bush. The range and scale of children's play are immeasurable. One of the adult witnesses, now a grandfather, remembers how his first interests comprehensively spanned his childhood world: the starry heavens and the dance of the ants in the dust, the dangers of climbing in the church belfry and the nest-building habits of the common wren. The living children whose play Sally Jenkinson so respectfully describes, in passages of great beauty and tenderness, are the most expert witnesses of all.

Sally Jenkinson invites her readers to follow this host of experts on their journey into adult life, travelling across the landscape of the imagination and through the playground of the mind. She urges us to recognise childhood in its own right as a place to be and become human, in the fullest sense of the word. The project of preparing for school, of getting ready to be a pupil, has no place in this geography of childhood; there are more important enterprises under way. More than once, the children in this book reminded me of the words of Christa Wolf, the great German novelist and essayist, who magnificently describes life's trajectory as the 'big Hope' – 'the long and never-ending journey towards oneself.' (In *The Search for Christa T* first published in 1968).

Sally Jenkinson's achievement is to establish beyond question the necessity and urgency of adult support for the succeeding generations of children undertaking this journey. Everyone who takes an interest in the lives of young children, in their being and becoming, will want to attend to what she is telling us. This is a beautiful and important book.

Cambridge, June 2001

Introduction

I wanted to write this book, which champions childhood and children's play, not out of a nostalgic or romantic conception of a lost golden age of the child (despite the inclusion of some retrospectives into childhood past), nor from a belief in the notion of an ideal childhood, but because I believe children today are experiencing an unprecedented degree of change in their lives; a level of change which threatens to undermine the stability of childhood and all that flows from it.

Glancing Back

Though child poverty affects an unacceptable one-third of British children today, in the 1950s and early 1960s, the majority of children suffered some form of material hardship. War had impoverished the country, and the larger families of those times practised prudence and ran tight budgets. Hand-me-down clothes, labelled not by image-conscious manufacturers, but by virtue of having being worn by older brothers and sisters, were the fashion of exigency, and children had different, more modest expectations. Paradoxically, restraint led to an abundance of creativity. Children worked hard at their play; entertainment was made, not bought; and young people created their own amusements. Necessity, that great spur to creativity, mothered some serious inventions. Trolleys, assembled from old pram chassis and their wheels – with bits of wood held perilously together by string, ingenuity and luck! – whizzed recklessly down streets, steered by boys with short trousers, bruised knees and triumphant expressions. Not a designer toy between them, those earlier charioteers owned the world.

Dolls of all shapes and sizes – though Barbie was not yet of their number – were washed, dressed, fed, and then wheeled around in battered miniature prams by solicitous or imperious mothers. Rag-dolls were exactly as their name suggests. Home-made boats, quickly crafted to seize the opportunity of a wet day's play, sailed down gutters at the pavement's edge. Bomb-sites were adventure playgrounds. There was danger, risk, and accident. There was also freedom to be.

Today's sophisticated, technological toys leave today's children very little room to be creative and original, only endlessly to repeat what has been done before. Now children are absent as cars dominate our streets, outdoor play is risky; children's designated play areas, with notable exceptions, are sanitized, safe and devoid of imagination. Our children are housebound, waiting for childhood to be over in order to gain some sense of freedom. In cocooned safety they watch television, video, play computers, and learn how to think, feel, and react to the world as they experience it – as it has been designed for them to experience. Sometimes it seems that packaged and passive childhood is the only kind on offer.

Although, statistically, children are no more likely to be abducted now than they were a century ago, the few tragic cases which do occur fuel parents' fears. In the past two decades, the amount of traffic has almost doubled on Britain's roads. Despite the introduction of traffic-calming measures, the very real threat to children remains. It is the same story in all technologically sophisticated societies. Smaller families mean that big sisters and brothers no longer take responsibility for their younger siblings, and children no longer roam in their own groups. These realities fuel fears which contribute toward the unprecedented curtailment of children's freedom. In an article aptly titled 'Swallows, Amazons … prisoners', Mary Ann Sieghart quotes Mayer Hillman (of the Policy Studies Institute, USA) who delivers an astonishing indictment on the state of childhood today:

> 'Children's lives have been evolving in a way that mirrors the lives of criminals in prison. They too have a roof over their heads, regular meals, and entertainment provided for them but they are not free to go out. Enforced detention, and restrictions on how they spend their time, are intended to seriously diminish the quality of their lives. But children are not criminals….'
>
> Mary Ann Sieghart[1]

Treating children in this way, says Mary Ann Sieghart – constraining their freedom as if they were indeed criminals – would be considered an infringement of rights if applied to adults. Children's time is almost always supervised and regulated by adults. There are few places for them to go to be away from us in safety. Our societies do not always suffer little children gladly. Adults are simultaneously children's protectors and their greatest detractors. Children learn to look to us for protection, yet they are also taught to fear us. A stranger is a potential source of danger, not someone to ask for help.

The Victorian child was seen and not heard; *today's children are neither seen nor heard.* As Cathy Nutbrown perceptively observes, there seems to be a rush to dispense with childhood, to reach its end, to scramble over its last fence, and ford its last stream as fast as possible:

'There is a sense of urgency about childhood – of hastening progress, of accelerating development. Is this born out of wanting the best for children or from some belief or value base which says the state of childhood is worth less than the state of adulthood and so we must do all we can to reach the day when childhood is over?... But children have their own pace and while, as adults, we pursue our own (and others') timescales and agendas, we need to be mindful of the need young children have to take their time. Pausing to listen to an aeroplane in the sky, stooping to watch a ladybird on a plant, sitting on a rock to watch the waves crash over the quayside – children have their own agendas and timescales, as they find out more about their world and their place in it: they work hard not to let adults hurry them and we need to hear their message.'

Cathy Nutbrown[2]

Childhood is, or should be, a state of grace, a big in-breath: both a 'being-here-now time' and a time of storing riches for the future. Have we lost the ability to empathize with children – to hear their voices, to enter their worlds? Can we protect them yet also leave them free?

This book is an attempt to climb back into the house of childhood, to catch again the dancing thoughts and feelings of our childhood. By remembering, we may be able to help our children find their way to their own hidden centre, to dance and play again in safety '...where life is still asleep under the closed flower...' (to quote the poet R. S. Thomas). We need to feel again that childhood is worthwhile; that it matters: now and for the future.

Charting a course

The image of the three boys in their boat, gazing far into the distance across the wide seas of their imagination, provides a useful metaphor for my theme. Life can be viewed as a journey, a voyage from childhood to the unknown land of the future. As parents, we do all we can to give our children strong and healthy bodies – we try to build vessels for them that are seaworthy and true. We equip our young sailors with provisions for the journey, with food, water, a radio, a compass to find their bearings, star charts to steer by, maps, rope, a lifejacket, a knife. We teach them the skills we think they will need. We try to anticipate all eventualities. We push them out to sea full of instructions and with a wealth of information distilled from our own earlier voyaging. We warn, cajole, and encourage. We launch them into the water with our best intentions, and with fluttering hopeful hearts. Yet though we do all this, we do well not to forget that the vision of the future they sail toward is uniquely their own, and that although we may share their past, the secret future always belongs to them. Every child carries the knowledge of who he or she wants to become, and charts their course to the new world guided by the deep wisdom and light of that inner vision.

Perhaps, looking at our boys in their battered old boat as they sail across the solid, green sea of grass in their kindergarten garden, we can see in our mind's eye other children in other places and at other times. We might even begin to remember our own great play dramas as we peered at possible futures for ourselves through the magical lens of the childhood imagination.

1. Beginnings

I spent a week in a Cotswolds village whilst writing this book. The owner of the converted dairy barn where I was staying had lived all his life in the leg end of a tiny, hidden village, to this day without shop or post office, a place that time seemed to have largely passed by. I asked him about his boyhood years in the 1950s and he generously opened the doors of his childhood to me. A country boy's story began to emerge, shyly and tentatively at first, but gradually growing stronger in the telling: a story of freedom and adventure bounded by spells of duty. His remarkable intimacy with the natural world – a world of remembered joys, delights and secrets – was revealed, as he shared the harvest of his childhood years with me

Jack was brought up by his grandmother, and together they ran the village dairy, supplying milk to local people and the village school. Jack's job was to milk the cows twice daily, once in the early hours of the morning, and again at four o'clock in the afternoon. Even when he and his little band of friends had roamed far from home – come what may, rain or shine – he would faithfully return each day at four o'clock for the afternoon milking session. Freedom and responsibility were not incompatible: each brought its own reward and was strengthened by its relationship to the other.

Jack's freedom was of a kind almost unimaginable today. He lived in a world where children were (relatively) safe on the streets.

His generation was the last to be free from thraldom to television; they were largely left in a state of 'healthy neglect' to make their own amusements where they could. And where couldn't they? The fields, woods, rivers, and lanes – all were theirs.

This is not to say that life was easy – far from it. It was just after the war, and there was little enough money to go round. Many children, including Jack, had family problems. Winters were cold, houses draughty; still to come were the luxuries of central heating, and resilience and resourcefulness were essential. Jack was never given a Christmas present; he never even had a toy. Yet, when he says, with a wistful look in his eye, 'We were outside boys', I see his younger self, the outside boy, fêted by an impossibly rich array of year-round gifts from nature. Every tree in the village was a friend, each barn owl flying home in the dusk was tracked by small intense eyes. All seasons were sweet to him. The large, weathered hand resting before me now once, in softer garb and smaller form, felt baby rabbits in their warm dark burrow; played finger-chase with the minnows in the stream; parted the branches to find the new-laid blackbird's egg, and steered a tin bath precariously down the narrow wind of the ice-carpeted main street.

His ear attuned itself to the sounds of nature; it learned discrimination and became a wise ear. His eye gazed at the star patterns in the vastness of night, and learned wonder. It followed the formation dance of the tiny ants at his feet, learned amazement, and became a wise eye. He read the world script long before the written word, and so became a wise boy. His heart became full and his head insightful. His feet found balance and his hands learned skills. His compass was the world.

Jack's play was also his learning. Although illegal today, in those days all the boys had egg collections. An instinctive lack of greed, borne from hardship and respect for life, made them refrain from removing more than one egg at a time from a clutch:

they were quick about their business, and always careful not to upset the mother bird who might desert if disturbed. No toys could have been cherished with greater reverence than were these sets of eggs. Muslin-brushed-white, delicate mint green, or palest cornflower blue, each brown-freckled little porcelain oval, a fragile but perfect signature of its type, had been carefully carried from field, barn, and wood to take its place with the others in a box or battered suitcase under a boy's bed.

Collections were both hard to build up and difficult to preserve: a desired egg could often involve a protracted and patient wait sometimes spanning the round of three seasons. Rough 'outside boys' though they were, they learnt to handle these nest-wrapped treasures with great care and tenderness, acquiring in the process the skills of classification and identification, and discovering new ways of improving their collections. For example, tiny eggs were very difficult to blow, usually cracking when pierced, or if they survived that, collapsing at the first puff of breath! The ever-resourceful boys discovered that when they were placed in ants' nests, the ants did a wonderful job scouring both inside and out, thus leaving the dainty seamless shells in pristine collector's condition: a natural deal brokered to benefit both boys and ants.

In giving primacy to adult knowledge, to our 'grown-up' ways of seeing the world, have we forgotten how to value other kinds of wisdom? Do we still care about the small secret corners of children's wisdom?

Jack's freedom to observe natural phenomena cultivated his interest and enthusiasm for things great and small, and helped develop his lively intelligence and enquiring mind. He smiled as he recalled a particularly baffling question. Whenever a wren's nest was found, it was almost always empty – there were dozens of empty nests yielding no eggs. Every spring, the same story. Why, he wondered? Did wrens have a special, crafty enemy ingenious enough to plunder eggs in a manner that escaped even their vigilance? He eventually found the answer to his question in a book on ornithology, an answer that finally solved the mystery and confirmed his own earlier empirical observations. Male wrens, it seems, are the architects and nest builders of the species. The cock bird builds a nest and offers it to the hen for inspection and approval. The discriminating female's approval, however, is not usually forthcoming, and so the poor male bird must continue to build until he finally manages to construct a nest which satisfies. The plethora of empty nests the boys had found were discarded examples of rejected sub-standard wren building.

In this little episode, I see Jack observing a phenomenon: a surfeit of eggless nests. I see him sustaining a question, and much later understanding a natural law (principle). No scientist could fault this process. Even now Jack retains this ability. He knows when the first swift arrives, could tell you what is happening down by the reeds at the river's edge, and not surprisingly is able to observe changes in the human landscape with the same eye for detail and astuteness. He reminds me that *looking is not always seeing,* and that our childhood is the time given to us to learn to see beyond the looking. He reaffirms the conviction that the consequences of good exploratory play are profound; that interest in all things, great and small, transposes into an attitude to life, a disposition of soul, if you will – a counterbalance to educated cynicism. And that freely exercising the capacity to 'wonder' lines the cradle of clear healthy thinking.

It is true to say that in their play, scientific discovery and dangerous living were pursued with equal vigour. There were rites of passage and rituals to fulfil. Climbing the tall church tower to scratch a nail-scored initial alongside those of past generations of daredevil boys in the lead roofing of the steeple base was a ritual reserved only for the bravest or most foolhardy of boys. Jack remembered his own ascent. With bated breath, he and a friend snaked their way through the spaces between the great ponderous church bells, terrified that one second's lapse of concentration – the merest touch of metal – would instantly clang out news of their whereabouts to the sleepy village below. Another pleasant danger was the river, which had a (safe) boy's hole and a (dodgy) man's hole – you learned to swim in the first and enjoyed your ability in the second. *No one had swimming lessons but everyone learned to swim.* Graduation from one hole to the other was sanctioned by those with mastery; their decisions determined fitness for passage.

Risk and danger were involved in these activities, and parents will balk at the more daring escapades. But this was a culture of childhood relatively free from adult intervention, where children challenged themselves at their own level, developing those competencies which were commensurate with their physical and mental stage – and not surprisingly, injury was a rare occurrence. The *self-selected* 'curriculum' avoided failure and loss of self-esteem, yet all their activities were underscored by an undeniable impetus to learn and to improve. Without formal gym or ballet classes, they learned to be fleet of foot and poised; they learned patience, cunning, and skill; they learned respect for the farmers whose fields they traversed and upon whose livelihoods their parents depended; they learned that kind of respect for each other which is free from rules. These were no helpless learners waiting for school to educate them, but small, skilled, purposeful human beings whose play had been the medium for their first lively education.

I asked Jack about his old friends. He told me that the friendships forged in his formative years had been crucial to his well-being at the time. When difficulties at home were too hard to bear, Jack's friends supplied the mainstay of gruff affection.

Loyal and tolerant, they each looked out for the other. Somewhat surprisingly, perhaps, to those familiar with William Golding's savage depiction of unsupervised children in *The Lord of the Flies,* there was no bullying. Conversely, the boys, and the occasional girl who drifted in and out of the group, tolerated weakness and encouraged each other. I was moved to hear that when these childhood friends meet each other, a look of familiarity, a nod of greeting is enough to reaffirm the abiding presence of a deep stratum of communal knowing; the bedrock laid down by a shared childhood which unites and binds them still. (These are the chosen *after school* friends of different ages and abilities – a motley band of disparate fellows. Our class, our age/peer cohort, holds quite a different place in our personal histories, or so it seems to me.)

Writing in 1969, Opie and Opie[3] acknowledge the importance of children's after-school play, as described above. They regret the formalizing of play and its introduction into the school curriculum. When children are institutionalized and herded together, they compete with each other, and their play can be markedly more aggressive than when they are in the street or in the wild places, they claim. Animals who are confined develop a pecking order, and it is often the toughest, and least sensitive animal that comes to the top. Then a process is established by which each animal takes revenge on the one next weakest to itself. In the wild, when fending for themselves, they are more 'civilized' – forced confinement brings out their 'animal' behaviour. Opie and Opie speak of the 'thoughtfulness and respect for the juvenile code' that they 'noted in the quiet places' during their research. Their plea is for the young to be given 'social space: the necessary space – or privacy – in which to become human beings'.[4]

The loss of childhood, in part a consequence of the insidious penetration of the media and its accompanying commercial market, is further compounded by the fact that in today's world there is little opportunity for children to play without adult supervision. 'Stranger danger', traffic, and other potential threats all conspire to keep children confined and restricted. As Mary Ann Sieghart writes in her article, 'Why can't boys and girls go out to play?'. 'Parks, streets and open fields have been replaced by computers, television and bedrooms. Adventures have to be experienced vicariously... Virtual freedom is the best that our children can hope for.'[5]

Jack's wonderful tale is, as he told it to me, unashamedly a *boy's* tale. But the argument for freedom to play, the main thrust of this book, applies in equal measure to both genders. For Jack and other children still fortunate enough to experience lively play, whether in urban or rural environments, each day can be a feast-day for the senses, the primary means by which the young learn. Our untutored senses enable us moment by moment, with breathtaking intensity, to become knowers of the world. Such a plenitude of knowledge in childhood – such gleeful learning! Our alert senses, at the peak of their powers of intelligence before conceptual frameworks intervene, stand at the threshold between ourselves and the world.

> *...And though you probe and pry*
> *With analytic eye,*
> *And eavesdrop all our talk*
> *With an amused look,*
> *You cannot find the centre*
> *Where we dance, where we play,*
> *Where life is still asleep*
> *Under the closed flower,*
> *Under the smooth shell*
> *Of eggs in the cupped nest*
> *That mock the faded blue*
> *Of your remoter heaven.*

R. S. Thomas, 'Children's Song' [6]

Poets have serenaded play in their verse. Painters have depicted its charms and pitfalls. Philosophers and educators have speculated on its meaning. Its mystery has beguiled us all through the centuries. In the remainder of this chapter I give a brief introduction to some of the theories of play which have informed our thinking in the past.

Historical Theories of Play: A Sketch

'The Platonic identification of play and holiness does not defile the latter by calling it play, rather it exalts the concept of play to the highest regions of the spirit. We said at the beginning that play was anterior to culture; in a certain sense it is also superior to it or at least detached from it. In play we may move below the level of the serious; but we can also move above it – in the realm of the beautiful and the sacred.'

John Huizinga[7]

The Greek philosopher **Plato** recognized the role of play in culture, ritual, and the sacred in human societies. He also recognized the close relationship between the creative play element and music, dancing, poetry, and art. It was Plato who famously described the 'play leap', the jumping, skipping, dancing, and joyful crying out of all young creatures who cannot keep their bodies still. Free movement and self-determined expression are the characteristics of play in the young.

In the mid-eighteenth century, the German poet, **Friedrich von Schiller** described play as the expression of exuberant energy and the origin of all art. In the nineteenth century, the English philosopher **Herbert Spencer** proposed a theory which owed much to Schiller's writings and to Darwin's *The Origin of Species*

(1859). Spencer's 'surplus energy' theory drew analogies between industrial processes, which he observed at the time, where pressure was seen to create surplus energy which needed an outlet, and exuberant children whose abundant energy also generated the need for an outlet. Bubbling away like little pressure cookers, children were sanctioned to 'let off steam' through the safety-valve of their play. Spencer also believed that levels of play increased proportionally according to a creature's place on the evolutionary ladder. Humans, at the top of the scale, were less dominated by the constant need for survival, and so possessed the highest levels of surplus energy forces, which then overflowed into play.

The American professor of psychology **G. S. Hall** (1884-1924), whose twin areas of study were education and evolution, was also influenced by Darwin's theories. Hall neatly combined the two disciplines in his 'recapitulation theory' of play. He based his theory on the notion that in embryonic development the child passes through all the stages from protozoan to human, or from fish-like creature to human, and that a child's individual development (ontogeny), follows the same pattern as that of the race (phylogeny). These observations were extended to embrace the whole of childhood. Hall claimed that as the embryo relives its ancient evolution, so too do children re-live, sequentially, the history of the race, re-enacting in their play behaviours which began with our prehistoric and primitive forebears. In their tribal wandering, and war and house-building games, children were seen to be recapitulating the activities of their ancestors.[8]

In the 1890s, **Karl Groos**, a professor of philosophy in Basle, wrote about animal and human play. He linked play with instinct, claiming that play trained animals for the roles they would play when mature. Animals lower down the scale have fewer skills, and those they have are of a very specialized and precise nature. Where instinctive patterns of behaviour predominate, for example in the insect world where survival is achieved through rigid patterns of behaviour and the use of specialized but limited skills, there is no need for play. Humans, however, must always be able to adapt to a changing world in ways which instinctive behaviours cannot anticipate. With fewer 'pre-programmed' or instinctive patterns of behaviour, humans have the greatest need to play in order to acquire further skills. A less strongly developed instinctive life allows experience rather than instinct to shape skills, which evolve to meet needs. Play is practice for life. Groos believed that the child learns by imitation and therefore needs a long period of protected childhood to practise the huge variety of skills required to be able to function successfully later in life.

At the turn of the last century, **Sigmund Freud**'s psychoanalytic theory linked behaviour to prior causes. He maintained that it is our feelings, emotions, and experiences which create behaviours. Nothing – or very little – in our behaviour happens by chance; hence the so-called Freudian slip. Children's play is determined by their experiences, both good and bad. Freud argued that the playing child uses objects to re-create pleasurable and unpleasant experiences from the real world. Seeking to compensate for painful encounters and to establish a return to equilibrium and pleasure, children determine their own play world to gain mastery of events, events over which in life they may have little or no control. They may give orders to their toys in play, whereas in real life they have no authority. Through play, the child becomes active rather than passive, reliving enjoyable experiences and resolving anxieties. Children want to be grown up, Freud observed, and they want mastery: in imitative play both these wishes can be fulfilled – if only temporarily. Freud regarded the process of stage-managing imaginative events, of 'day dreaming', as the forerunner to the development and production of art. Play, he suggested, was one of the means of achieving pleasure. He regarded the pursuit of pleasure and the avoidance of pain as prime motivators in life.[9]

The Swiss psychologist **Jean Piaget** was interested in the development of children's reasoning at various stages. Central to his theory of intellectual development were the complementary processes of assimilation and accommodation. At a basic level, assimilation is the process by which the world is made part of the organism. When we digest food, we assimilate it and make it part of ourselves. In the same way, information is internalized, assimilated, and made use of for the individual's own purposes. Assimilation features in children's symbolic play where objects are given personal meanings to suit the player. Accommodation occurs when the organism adapts itself to the external world. When we bend down to avoid a low ceiling, we are accommodating ourselves to the contours of the world. Optimal learning takes place when these two processes are in a state of equilibrium. *Play* occurs when what is already known through assimilation predominates. *Imitation* occurs when accommodation predominates and the child adjusts itself to the world in order to take on new information. Through assimilation and accommodation children organize their own thinking and adapt themselves to new information. Play and imitation are fundamental in the development of intelligence and social adaptation, and feature throughout Piaget's account of the stages of logical development.[10]

Erik Erikson, writing in the 1970s and drawing on psychoanalytical theory and clinical experience, observed that children's play reflected the themes, interests, and anxieties current in their lives. The play worlds they created were metaphors for their lives, and featured their main concerns, interests, worries, and preoccupations. By means of longitudinal research, he also came to the surprising conclusion that their later 'adult lifestyles had also been implicit in the themes of their childhood play.'[11] He claimed that individuals are always partners with their futures, and that play not only reveals the present but [amazingly] also prefigures the future.[12] In their different ways both Froebel and Steiner also subscribed to this view (see page 51).

Play is mischievously difficult to pin down. The word itself is resistant to categorization, as the historian and writer **John Huizinga** wryly observed in his scholarly and influential book *Homo Ludens* (1950): '... [Is not] the act of playing... of such a peculiar and independent nature as to lie outside the ordinary categories of action?'[13] Playing, he explains, is not doing. You do not 'do' a game as you might do ironing, woodwork, or ballet; you play it. Huizinga also describes play as an 'interlude', separate from the everyday, from our immediate satisfaction of wants and appetites, and as 'adorning and amplifying' life.[14] He also describes it as integral to life! – thus posing an interesting paradox about the existential nature of play. How can something outside life be, at the same time, integral to it?

Finally, **Friedrich Froebel** (1782-1852) and **Rudolf Steiner** (1861-1925) also had important insights into the nature of play, as did **Margaret Lowenfeld**, writing in the 1930s. Their various ideas will feature in later sections of this book.

No one theory provides a comprehensive rationale of play but all of them express part of the truth about it and contribute enormously to our understanding of its many mysteries. The following chapters examine play in more detail – and look at the consequences of its absence. Current thought places great emphasis on the *social* aspects of play, and the next chapter will highlight the importance of children's social play.

2. Let's Play! – The Social Value of Play

Why Does Play Matter? – and Can It Help Us to Get on with Each Other?

After studying play in animals and humans for many years, the American psychiatrist Dr Stuart Brown has come to the conclusion that childhood play, rather than being peripheral or optional, is *central* to an individual's healthy development, and to the development of his or her social relationships and status. Play is as important to life as is sleeping and dreaming, he maintains. Much of Brown's work concerns what he calls 'the dark side of play' – the implications of its absence.

Dr Brown's initial interest in the consequences of a play-less childhood was sparked by a behavioural study into the background of 25-year-old Texan student, Charles Whitman. In 1966, Whitman climbed to the top of his university tower and opened fire on the people below, killing 13 and wounding 31, before himself being fatally wounded by the police. Brown discovered that as well as evidence of abuse and violence in Whitman's childhood, there was also another less obvious but no less compelling finding. This was *the absence of a normal pattern of play*. Charles Whitman was described by his teachers as a 'frightened little kid *who never played spontaneously*'. At home, the boy was under the total control of his father and had almost no time to play, even by himself.

This discovery led Stuart Brown to look into the history of other criminals. One study of 26 convicted murderers showed that in no less than 90 per cent of cases there had been abnormal patterns of play (for example, violent, aggressive play) in childhood; that there was either an absence of play, or that some form of abnormal play behaviour had taken place. This and other subsequent research provided Brown with the evidence he needed to make a convincing argument in support of children's play. He has since widened his field of study and found a further correlation between brilliant adult thinkers and excellent childhood players. Understandably, he believes play to be a powerful and positive force for the good.[15]

Play can be a powerful diagnostic tool as well as a therapeutic agent. We adults need to notice our children's play, be brave enough not to deny or forbid it, and try to respect the child's need for it. Without over-analysing what is played out before us, it may be that, with sensitivity and tact, we can offer help and healing – should warning signs appear. Violent play in a traumatized child, who is usually subject to raging feelings, for example, can be worked through in a positive way.

Brown's findings stressed the importance of *spontaneous* play. Much play in nurseries today is *teacher*-directed, and 'wrapped around' a learning objective, and free time is often *adult*-controlled, which is not the same as child-initiated spontaneous play.

Stuart Brown also makes some interesting parallels between animal play and human interactions. He describes a meeting in the frozen area of the Hudson Bay, Manitoba, between a lean and hungry 1,200 pound polar bear and a dog chained to a kennel. As the bear lumbered toward the dog, observers felt certain that the poor dog was destined to become the bear's lunch. The dog, however, saw the polar bear's approach as an opportunity for play and began to exhibit play signals: head on one side, tail wagging, and so on. Although dogs and bears are traditional enemies, play signals are usually so clear and unambiguous that they are capable of crossing species lines. To everyone's surprise, the polar bear accepted the cues and gave his own play signals in return. The dog and the bear played together for a week, the bear returning for further sessions each day. The point Brown makes is that the bear willingly limited his immense strength and presumably his hunger *for the good of the game.* His natural aggression was reined in – he bit gently to match his strength to that of the dog. Limiting strength, controlling aggression, impulse control, are all exercised in play. Biting too hard transgresses the rules of the game.

'Maturity in a playful species creates the ability to integrate oneself in lightness with nature and the world… Play in action, it seems to me, among its other virtues regards life as sacred. It doesn't kill or dominate, it handicaps the strong with the weak, it crosses species lines… it evokes peace and security and avoids true violence.'

Stuart Brown[16]

Children also make up their own rules and agree to abide by them for the good of the game. This is pre-cultural behaviour. The Russian psychologist Lev Vygotsky, recognized play as an essential agent in the maturation process of the child. In *Early Childhood Education,* Tina Bruce writes: 'Vygotsky believes that when children are involved in imaginative play they will renounce what they want, and willingly subordinate themselves to rules, in order to gain the pleasure of the play. He argues that in play they exercise their greatest self-control'.[17] How different in character is this activity from the alienated world of the bedroom TV-watcher, whose desires are instantly gratified as programmes are turned off and on at will, and whose *self*-control is replaced by its bogus counterpart, *'remote* control'. The ability to renounce our desires for others is the bedrock of truly social behaviour – with the development of relationships and appropriate emotional responses. The capacity to share and to take on the perspective of the other is all played out in germinal form in the multiplicity of games which children in all cultures play in their early years.

Brown also describes the play of a badger witnessed by a colleague. The badger's normal activities were instinctive. He was in either 'fight' or 'flight' mode. In both these states of being, his behaviour was inflexible and very difficult to change. In play mode, however, the badger developed new actions – somersaults, slides, skids; he was flexible and adaptive, and his mood could be altered. Brown suggests that inflexible animal behaviour has a relationship to dogmatic human behaviour: people who are inflexible and fixed are acting from a rigid paradigm. The play paradigm, however, is more flexible and able to change to meet changing circumstances. Although play patterns vary across the species and each species has its own way of playing – all lambs leap, for example – *each animal exhibits something individual and original within its own play.* Released from the constraints of instinctive/compulsive behaviour, a certain freedom to act individually is then possible.

Sara Smilansky, an Israeli researcher who has studied play in Israel and the USA since the 1960s, found that what she labelled 'sociodramatic play' was an accurate indicator of social competence. Dramatic play occurs when a child takes on a role, usually imitating someone they have seen in a given situation. When children play dramatic games *together,* they are engaged in sociodramatic play. A further refinement of Smilansky's definition is *thematic fantasy play,* in which children play fictional situations they have never seen but only imagine. The central element in dramatic and sociodramatic play is *imitation,* claims Smilansky: '...which paradoxically establishes a reality level for children. They try to act, talk, and look like some real adult person and recreate situations that are in their perception real.'[18] Imitation combines with make-believe and imagination as children fill in the gaps of their experience and begin creating stories. In this kind of play children interact with each other in play episodes, they learn to persist in a role, they communicate verbally about what is happening, and they use objects symbolically (a basket, or circular bread board might become a steering wheel).

Smilansky argues that skilled sociodramatic players are more successful in all fields and are better at school integration. She gives eight compelling reasons in support of sociodramatic play: [19]

1. It demands the intellectual discipline of taking on appropriate behaviour for the role selected. (How do I behave as a nurse/ spaceman/baby? I need to represent my role so that others can recognize my character.)
2. The child needs to grasp the essence of a play situation – the major features of a game. (What is necessary to include in playing a sailing game, for example, and what is not?)
3. Playing to a given theme teaches concentration. (I must be convincing and consistent over a period of time in my role, so I concentrate on it and immerse myself in it.)
4. Participation in sociodramatic play requires children to discipline their actions to fit in with the narrative and the roles they have assumed. (The dog [my character] may want to speak, but a speaking dog may be outside the imaginative terms of this game. The dog role requires communication 'in dog', so expressive gestures and sounds must be used – and the limitations imposed upon my human speech are accepted as a challenge.)

5. The story line can change with the input of others, teaching the child flexibility: there may be more than one right way to do things.

6. Play gives new approaches to problems and new concepts. 'For example, the child may learn that there may be other behaviour patterns for "father" than those with which he or she is familiar.'

7. The child moves toward abstract thought and symbolism. Smilansky's explanation is worth quoting here:

'We may observe the following procedure: the child begins with a toy that inspires imitative play – for example, a toy typewriter – and the child pretends to write a story. After a while, owing to the rapidity of spontaneous play and its growing complexity, the child substitutes a box or an anonymous chunk of wood for the toy typewriter. Later, having misplaced the wood, the child uses a gesture, perhaps drumming the fingers in the air. Finally, dispensing with the actions altogether, the child simply announces the writing of a story.'[20]

8. Children who are accomplished sociodramatic players understand different interpretations and roles and different definitions of various situations and themes, both in school work and in a wider context. (In school work, active participation in new thought-worlds is a necessary part of learning. When playing together children teach each other to embrace difference; they imagine and play out different realities to their own.)

Success in sociodramatic play, skill in the use of good interventions, good interactions, and flexibility all develop social competence and prepare the child not only for integration into school but also for life itself. Good players learn to take their cue from others; are prepared sometimes to lead and sometimes follow, and, crucially, are willing to learn; *to change, to adapt, and to move on.*

Stuart Brown's colleague, the play expert Bob Fagan, identifies the deep connection between play and evolution. 'In a world continuously presenting unique challenges and ambiguity, play prepares them for an evolving planet.'[21] Play is ambiguous, exciting, risky, challenging, and compelling precisely because of its unpredictability. A game's outcome, like the future, is a mystery. Play prepares children to enter the game of life without undue fear.

Smilansky also found that disadvantaged children played less sociodramatic, thematic and fantasy games, which further disadvantaged them because they failed to learn to play 'the school game'. They were less creative and showed fewer skills in intelligence and socially. School work requires imagination, so prominent in games of make-believe. By living into play fantasies, the ground is prepared for new problems. How do others live? What was it like in Ancient Greece? Can I imagine a story to write? Fantasy games also require good verbal skills. The 'pre-eminence of language' in sociodramatic play, Smilansky says, 'cannot be overlooked in evaluating its significance for later achievements and success in school.'[22]

As I write, a letter has arrived describing one pre-schooler's dramatic, but not yet sociodramatic, school game. In the game, she is Mr Roberts, the school bus driver (who does exist), and her dollies are the pupils, whom she is driving to school. They are all sitting in neat rows on the school bus and she turns to look at them, drives, and makes conversation. This kind of play is wonderfully satisfying on so many levels. It is fun. It is an artistic re-creation of a scene observed and therefore has aesthetic merit. It allows 'physical or external thinking' at a stage when the child's own mental processes are not sufficiently developed for abstract thought, and it rehearses a situation to be encountered in the future – giving emotional reassurance.

I watched some girls playing 'Home' recently. As in many homes, there was no 'dad' in this game. An overwrought mother, a baby, and two big sisters lived in a house made of clothes horses and cloths. 'The mother', overworked and exhausted, imitated almost the full range of adult stress gestures; hands on hips, then in the air in exasperation; big sighs; looks of desperation; shaking of the head; raising of the eyebrows. Her selection of appropriate emotional responses to the imagined situation was impressive – and moving. She told the big sisters, who took all their cues for their behaviour from her play, that she needed to go shopping and that they should look after the baby. When she returned, she was even more stressed, and told the big sisters that it was no good, they would have to leave home – she couldn't cope. The big sisters then made Dick Whittington-style bundles for their belongings, waved goodbye to their 'mother' and left home. They were imitating, and also, it appeared, genuinely feeling sadness. The girls ended up with nowhere to live and were forced to sleep on the streets. The two homeless girls unwrapped their bundles and forlornly bedded down for the night together, each gaining comfort from the other.

The above game was a mini tragedy, played out with great intensity and depth of feeling. Each child was imitating and exploring a reality not her own. In the make *believe* of their game they were busy discovering important truths about big themes – responsibility, parenting, decision-making, love, loss, companionship and strength in adversity.

The importance of imitation in children's play, as illustrated above, cannot be over-emphasized. It is imitation, which establishes Smilansky's 'shared reality level for children'.[23] Where limitations of experience prevent faithful imitation, make-believe or imagination enter, enabling children to explore the truths of other realities together. In the game of leaving home, known elements from life were faithfully imitated from memory and others were creatively imagined.

Through sociodramatic play, using imitation, children create life situations/dramas based on their own experiences, usually involving domestic scenarios; and in thematic fantasy play, which is more like a fictional story, children learn to acknowledge, grasp, and take on the perspectives of others. Through role play, children learn to adjust their play to that of their partner, and in so doing broaden their understanding and increase their social skills.

Role play requires choice and acceptance. There is role giving (including to the self) and role receiving. 'I'm the mummy', says one four year old to no-one in particular, as she starts her game – possible 'children' begin to show an interest. 'Pretend I'm an egg and you laid me', says a boy to his friend in one of the most amazing opening lines I have ever heard. The first is an example of self-directed role play, the second requires acceptance from the designated egg-layer, who must make some pretty swift decisions before the game can proceed: what am I – a hen, an alligator, a Griffin? What do I do next? Often, considerable negotiation precedes a game. Negotiation is at the heart of social competence and contract: for the good of the game, or for the happiness of the other, I agree to terms less favourable to me. I might agree to play the little sister, although I really want to be the parent.

Connolly and Doyle found that

'…the amount and complexity of children's fantasy play were significantly correlated with four measures of social competence: teacher rating of social skill; peer popularity; affective role-taking ability; and amount of positive social activity (e.g. expressions of friendship, invitations to play and amount of conversation)'.[24]

The more imaginative the games that children play together, and the greater the complexity of their play, the stronger the indication that they will also develop higher levels of social competence, and interpersonal (i.e. knowing and communicating with others) and intrapersonal (i.e. self knowledge and management) skills.

For play to function successfully, shared definitions and agreement over what is permissible within a particular game need to be established. Two boys were heard having a conversation about whether or not the house, which they had already built, could or could not become a castle; after *lengthy* deliberations, they finally reached mutual agreement and decided that it could. (These important social negotiations just don't happen at a solitary desk or work-table.)

A piece of wood becomes a skilfully played saxophone in which the child's gestures faithfully re-create the original observation, down to the smallest detail. Children create a succession of 'worlds' which, though sometimes fantastic, nevertheless represent a coherent whole, each with its own symbol structure and appropriate set of props. In one kindergarten, a particular spot was usually chosen to function as the doorway in a variety of different versions of the game of 'House'. This threshold became the agreed *sign* and symbol of boundary and ownership. The sanctity of the door, as the central sustaining feature in games of 'House', seems to be a universally recognized feature. Entry by any other route is simply not permitted; if children do start coming in through the walls, it usually signals the breakdown of the game. This was one of many self-imposed 'rules' which were accepted by the group. A series of more tangible props was also used to support play activity. In the syntax of their play these physical props functioned as instant, adaptable, and supremely interchangeable metaphors: conkers became matches; string, snakes; a hand-sized piece of wood a mobile-phone.

Despite so much evidence in support of play, it is the competitive work ethos that rules in both the UK and in the

United States. Academic success, it is believed, can only be secured by an early start at school. Play is either given low status or put to use as an agent for cognitive functions – with its multiple benefits thereby being ignored. This seems like folly. We know that cohesive societies are built upon higher-order social skills. We know that social play develops those skills, and yet play is under threat from all quarters. In preventing play, we tread a perilous path toward an uncertain future.

An experienced and long-serving head of a first school expressed her sadness at the advent of four year olds who lack social skills. She felt they were desperately deprived because they did not know how to communicate with others, or to share, and were unable to care for anybody or anything. They ran around aimlessly in the playground and were often aggressive. Lacking social skills these children became increasingly alienated.

Play and Cultural Access

Sociodramatic play can anticipate social roles of the future and reflect rituals and customs, institutions, and the way children are treated in their societies. The researchers Curry and Arnaud[25] looked at cross-culture perspectives on sociodramatic play. They found that although the themes were universal, the character of play varied according to cultural tradition. The two researchers compared the play of children in five different North American cultures: Appalachian children from West Virginia: Mexican Americans in Texas: Southern Black children in Texas; Native Americans in Montana; and city children of mixed socio-economic background in Western Pennsylvania. They analysed film of these groups of children's dramatic play and observed that in all cultures children acted out the following common themes:

- Nurturance and domestic play based on food preparation and feeding;

- Family relationships and roles such as mother/baby inter-actions and the roles of fathers and siblings;
- Representations of the children's physical and human environment using blocks and miniature life toys;
- Relationships between medical personnel and patients;
- Play based on aggressive themes and frightening happenings involving monsters, accidents, and the like.

Curry and Arnaud found

> '...clear differences in play styles, emphases and cultural content. The children in the five groups also built quite different representations of their surroundings (e.g. coal mines, farms, corrals, super highways, cities and rural villages) and enacted different adult occupations related to their own experiences (e.g. animal auctioneers and butchers, miners, rural medical personnel, Native American dancers)'.[26]

I find these unsentimental observations both scientifically interesting and also powerfully moving. The unwitting testimony revealed in the intimacy of the researchers' list gives a rare and unsentimental insight into the child's world. It is a distillation of the 'every child' experience.

Everychild: 'What Do I Play?'

> 'My nurture; my family; my physical and social situation; my health, my illness, and my pain; my strength and weakness; my fears both real and imaginary. I also play my love and loving; gifts and giving. These are my issues, my world. This is me: the universal child, your child. Can you see me? Hear me?'

Ecce Homo. Behold also the child.

Children want to understand life, to feel the moral fabric of society, and to access their culture. They want to work out what makes people tick. In *The Kindness of Children,* Vivian Paley quotes a school director, who asks: 'And what do the children philosophize about?' His answer: 'How to gain access to every person, feeling, thing and event.'[27]

I witnessed cultural access in action in the shopping games of some children in a kindergarten in York. Both real and pretend shopping requires specific cultural knowledge, and playing shops authentically involves many skills. This really was authentic play!

A wiser person might have just watched, but I decided to join in. I made my bid for entry by asking whether I could buy something. I was told irritably that I would need money of course. Of course, obvious, really – but where was money exactly? Money was in the bank, 'over there', said the shop assistant gesturing with a sweep of her arm, toward some shelves behind me. Returning, I offered my conkers, which I had (wrongly) assumed to be money. 'That's not money', she said with disdain, 'shells are, of course'. Of course! After another trip to the bank and now finally equipped with the right currency – some small shells and a large flat one – I returned for another try. 'I'd like some potatoes please', I said. Grudgingly, my potatoes (these were conkers) were put into a little bag. Then came a surprise. The bag was held at waist level, and then moved across the work surface with slow deliberation. As it was held and moved in this formalized way, a perfectly synchronized 'beep' accompanied the mid-point of the transaction. My purchase had been scanned! I had hardly registered my amazement when I was asked to hand over my credit card: the flat shell. This was expertly swiped through an invisible machine and I was asked, with the hint of a smile, to sign the payment slip. The game continued as I moved on and I noticed the queue growing.

I was inspired by the girl's mastery of the situation. The level of knowledge based on her own free observations and intuitions,

25

which she was able to bring to her play-creation, was remarkable. She was scripting, acting, directing, and performing the play as it was happening. The serious business of modern shopping had been faithfully re-created down to the smallest detail. Those small eyes and ears waiting at the check-out counter in the real shop had missed nothing. Here were children finding ways to access their culture and to master it. By using representation and imagination, they were living into the rules and rituals of purchase. Though they owned nothing at the end of the game, their richness of understanding and ability to act in the world had increased dramatically. So had mine.

In Sri Lanka, Prosser et al:

> '...saw children acting out a home sequence, with a boy taking the role of father who was supposed to be going to work. The girl, taking the role of mother, gave instructions like, "you must serve the father first and a lot of food must be given to him". Here is an instance of the father's role being clearly defined, reflecting the cultural values of that society.'[28]

In both the above examples, distinct cultural norms were being enacted as the children imitated and tried to gain access to their respective cultures. Play provides children with a 'shared reality level', which unites them, transcending custom, gender and even language barriers. It also respects and indeed celebrates difference and offers opportunities for new learning and cultural exchange. In its inclusiveness, play prevents prejudice and creates a more tolerant society.

Henry Bett, author of *The Games of Children,* written in 1929 when there were still plenty of children's games to see in street and field, felt that nothing was more characteristic of the child than the faculty of imitation. He noted that, in many instances, the imitation dated back to earlier epochs in human history. He wrote:

'Among the [American] Indians to-day it is stated that the games of the adults generally are played ceremonially, as pleasing to the gods, and with the purpose of securing fertility, causing rain, expelling demons, and so on. It is likely that the children in prehistoric times imitated all the other doings of their elders, so that it is possible that some children's games are the ghosts of these ancient mysteries.'[29]

This indicates a cultural/spiritual heritage of deep significance; and images of the silent but monumental ring game(s) being 'played out' at Stonehenge and other ancient sites across the globe come to mind.

The children's game 'Sally Go Round the Sun' seems to resonate with echoes of our distant past. It is both an intimation and an imitation of an older solar/lunar mystery which reminds us of our abiding relationship to the cosmos, the sun, and the moon.

Children have a sure instinct for the theatre of ritual, the magic of mystery, and the sense of the moment. In the preface to her book *The Traditional Games of England, Scotland and Ireland,* Alice Gomme also points out that in a large proportion of their games children are involved in the activity of imitating or mimicking the adults around them. She writes: 'In many of these games we have, there is little doubt, unconscious folk dramas of events and customs which were at one time being enacted as part of the serious concerns of life before the eyes of children many generations ago.'[30]

In the traditional game 'Round and Round the Village', the children create a little 'village' of houses by standing together and holding hands. Gomme describes this activity as forming 'the rudiments of community'.[31] The children then pass around the boundary of the 'village' and wander in serpentine fashion in and out of the 'windows'. The players act as 'chorus' by describing, in the words they sing, the actions of those performing their parts.

The narrative in this game is one of marriage, and as Gomme indicates, the 'burden' of the game rests with the line, 'As we have done before'. Marriage is a recurring event, and this game, and many others like it, symbolize continuity. They belong to the body of games called 'custom games', where 'children act in play what their elders do seriously'.[32] Through the re-creation of these *rites de passage* children gradually come to understand the world and its ways. The literal meaning of the word 'recreation,' now used to denote sporting or leisure activities, is to 'create anew'.

In my kindergarten a five-year-old boy had been to a wedding over the weekend, which his mother privately told me had made a tremendous impact upon him. Out of the corner of my eye, I saw that he was already busy in the dressing-up box. I wondered whether he would re-create his experience and, if so, what he would select and reject in order to reinvent the scene. He was an inventive and imaginative boy: only the week before he had wound himself tightly in swathes of green muslin to become a caterpillar. His play was always totally convincing. The caterpillar was so well bound that – once he had navigated the entire kindergarten floor on his tummy – he had to be helped back to human form, his arms and legs having been rendered immobile by the binding. This particular day, he had chosen to wear a white polo neck to school. He selected a deep red tabard to go over a cream robe. With his white, round collar, red and cream robe, and serious demeanour, he effected an immediate transformation. He waited shyly for me to see him and then smiled. The magic was complete. The dignity of the office of priest in his chasuble, which he had observed, and which had so impressed him, was stunningly re-created in the midst of the bustle of a busy kindergarten room. Nursery teachers and parents everywhere will have had similar experiences.

In play, a child becomes something of a philosopher: to play well, he needs to grasp the necessary conditions sufficient to re-create his experience convincingly. The boy above had assembled his re-creation sparingly but with great accuracy. The ability to pare down to the essentials is a transferable skill – useful in art, writing, surgery, or engineering. To quote Smilansky more fully:

> 'Playing a role demands enough intellectual discipline to include only behaviour appropriate for the role the child has taken on. The child must judge and select from a pool of possibilities…, must grasp the major features of a character or a theme, the central characteristics.'[33]

The creative player applies intellectual discipline and becomes culturally enabled.

Absent Adults: A Supportive Framework for Children's Play

> 'We have managed to eradicate many of the negative elements but we have also lost many of the positive ones…. The absence of adults, social and existential insecurity, pulverisation of values, a crumbling belief in the future [affect children who become] passive, tired and indifferent.'
>
> Reidun Iverson[34]

In traditional communities, children would play and work at their own chores alongside adults. Tina Bruce calls this the apprenticeship model. In complex post-industrial societies like ours, children and adults are increasingly separated. Nowadays working adults are largely absent from their children's lives. Children hardly ever see adults at work and must quite rightly wonder, 'What exactly do adults do?' Bruce draws attention to the traditions of hunting, gathering, and agricultural societies, noting that: 'Children learn through…

watching, playing, socialising and slowly doing.... In their play, they reflect on these active experiences and wallow in them...[35]

Learning to do what they have observed in the company of adults flies in the face of current educational practice, which fills children full of abstract, de-contextualized learning, and alienates them from shared activity with adults. Bruce questions the logic of putting children through ever longer and more rigorous hours of schooling in terms of their total development – a practice which results in the erosion of their free flow or 'wallowing' time, the time for actively reflecting on their experiences through play.

In Steiner kindergartens and in other settings where early academic pressure has less of a hold, the tradition of embracing children in adult work is still maintained. Cleaning, cooking, baking, gardening adults accompany the children and invite them to participate in real, observable work. Exposure to adult work helps develop good habits and is a tremendous incentive to play. So much work is carried out unseen by sophisticated machines these days that children have little opportunity to see human hands doing more than button-pushing. In my own experience, adult work functions as a great energy boost to children: it is an antidote to apathy, and even if their play apparently has no connection to the work they see, it becomes noticeably richer after exposure to it. Whether they join in or not, and that choice is always left free in a Steiner setting, their own activities are swept up, as it were, and energized by the brush of the adult broom.

Working adults of the past had little time to play with their children. Today, we think it is our duty to play with our children, rather than to work with them, and we rush to finish our tasks so that we can have 'quality time with the kids'. Entering shared reality levels together in play can be enormous fun, but children nearly always play best when left to their own devices, in, or just out of, the shadow of the working adult. Because we are always so busy, the involving of our children in our work, especially when they helpfully unmake the beds we have just made, can seem difficult. It probably requires a more relaxed attitude to house-keeping and a more tolerant attitude toward child-keeping. Beds can always be remade – children can't.

The illustration of the boys at the seashore (see photo below) demonstrates this kind of relaxed play, which clearly reflects the interests of a fishing community. Steve Biddulph, author of *Raising Boys*, highlights the loss of adult men as role models for boys; and the same is also arguably becoming true for girls in relation to their mothers (which is not to deny, of course, that men can model feminine qualities, and vice versa).

The sense of community, which went beyond the family, is weaker than ever before. Poignant reminders remain in the ring games still occasionally played today. 'Round and Round the Village' is one such game.

Clearly, there were negative elements in the past, including rigid authority, neglect, hard labour, lack of certain freedoms, and abuses of power, as Reidun Iverson[36] points out, but in pre-industrial society children were with adults in their work places

and there was time for outdoor play. In contrast, anxiety, tension, intellectual overloading, abstract explanations, too early a demand on memory and understanding – all symptoms of our speed-dominated society – serve to weaken play and put stresses on the child.

If the adult world lacks dimension and depth, a paucity of rich experience for the child to imitate will result. Children need substance upon which to put their culture to work in order to transform and remake the world in their own way. In our media-drenched society – a world of simulacra and superficiality, where the characters of the TV soap opera 'Neighbours' are as real, or in some cases more real, than the people who live next door – our offerings to the child are not always beautiful, good, or true, and often fall short of being worthy of imitation. Children are natural fisher-folk – they cast their nets wide; just what the 'catch' of their early years will be depends in significant part upon us.

The trawl of childhood involves the feelings. It is not only the head, as Pascal observed, but also the heart which has its reasons. The central role of play in the development of a rich feeling life and emotional adjustment is the theme for the next chapter.

3. Teaching the Heart: The Emotional Value of Play

'I sincerely believe that for the child, and for the parent seeking to guide him, it is not half so important to know as to feel. If facts are the seeds that later produce knowledge and wisdom, then the emotions and the impressions of the senses are the fertile soil in which the seeds must grow. The years of early childhood are the time to prepare the soil. Once emotions have been aroused – a sense of the beautiful, the excitement of the new and the unknown, a feeling of sympathy, pity, admiration or love – then we wish for knowledge about the object of our emotional response. Once found it has lasting meaning. It is more important to pave the way for the child to want to know than to put him on a diet of facts he is not ready to assimilate.'

Rachel Carson[37]

The current emphasis on formal learning, and over-use of mediated experiences – television, video, computer games – can deprive children of immediate sensory encounters with the real world. Play provides the opportunity for a smorgasbord of wonderful first-hand experiences. Dry knowledge = bored learners.

In nature play, in which all the senses are active, a correspondence of feeling within the child, a symphony of responses to the world, is aroused. Our first feelings are educated by our senses, for it is the senses that begin the task of articulating and differentiating the feelings.

The immediacy of our childhood experiences offers a communion with the world and the opportunity for gaining wisdom and intuition unfettered by the intellect. Our early loves linger, as George Eliot poignantly observed:

> 'Life did change for Tom and Maggie and yet they were not wrong in believing that the thoughts and loves of these first years would always make part of their lives. We could never have loved the earth so well if we had had no childhood in it.... What novelty is worth that sweet monotony where everything is known and loved because it is known.... Our delight in the sunshine on the deep bladed grass today, might be no more than the faint perception of wearied souls, if it were not for the sunshine and the grass in the far-off years, which still live in us and transform our perception into love.'[38]

The threads of our childhood perceptions filter upward and become integrated into our personalities. Our futures are built on our present perceptions, and the quality of our early encounters with the world have the greatest and most lasting influence over us. Deep knowledge, deep concentration, deep play bring deep satisfaction and contentment with life.

Can we imagine ourselves back into that place of discovery when the world was new, to that time when we were thrilled by our senses? Are we able to recapture the intense curiosity we had about the fascinating world in which we found ourselves, and can we empathize with those who inhabit that state of being now?

Whenever a child is physically doing – and much of young children's doing is bound up with their play – they are also feeling. Wet sand is not just a concept; it is an *experience,* causing an inner sensation, a *reaction*. Action and reaction. Sand between the fingers, sand in the mouth, rasping around, over and under the tongue, and cracking between the teeth, is different from sand in the shoes. Dry, warm, flowing sand is different from cold, wet, clumping sand. Yet these experiences are all sand. Sand *experienced,* as opposed to 'taught about or explained', is known, felt, and understood. Sand is not reduced to a concept but a series of enlightening encounters; a conversation between the senses and the thing sensed. Life through feeling and doing becomes subtle and paradoxical: sand is hard *and* soft, lumpy *and* liquid. In all its mutability, there are many truths about sand.

Through healthy use of their senses, children first learn to understand oppositions between things; they learn subtlety and gradation and begin to build a personal feeling life: a sensory memory. A richly orchestrated sense life helps create a heterogeneous emotional life, which in turn creates a differentiated life of thought. This paves the way for a discerning adult response to the world.

Speaking at an Alliance for Childhood conference in Brussels in September 2000, Craig Kielberger, the 17-year-old founder of the international organization 'Free the Children', in which no officer is older than eighteen, said that the purpose of education should be 'to teach young people *to react to the world'*. He began his work after browsing through the weekend paper in search of the comic section and coming across an article on child slavery which made an overwhelming impression upon him. He *reacted* by setting up an organization with his school friends to alleviate child suffering. Now leading a huge operation that has had great success in its work for children, Craig himself is an exemplar of what it means to react, and respond to the world.

The slow acquisition of a language of feelings begins at birth. Watch the look on a baby's face when a new and unexpected taste is introduced for the first time. The reaction is total, the entire little body resonates with the experience. Our adult senses, in contrast, are easily dulled – the amount of beauty, suffering, noise to which we have become insensitive or immune is staggering. We need artists, poets, and writers to help us feel again, to re-educate *emotions,* those moving feelings that have become stilled.

Daniel Goleman places great emphasis on the development of the feelings. In his valuable book *Emotional Intelligence,* he suggests that our current view of intelligence is far too narrow, and that in fact emotional 'literacy'[39] plays a far greater role in our success as adults than we realize. Our own rich life of feeling enables us to feel empathy for others (see page 45 for a fuller account).

Children Explore Their Feelings through Play

Play is the perfect stage for the theatre of feelings to find expression. Playing out the dramas resting on their own hearts can be a journey of understanding for children – about their own feelings and about those of others. The intensity of children's feelings, as many heart-rending autobiographies testify, should not be underestimated. Janusz Korczak,[40] author and friend to children, who died with the children in his care at the Treblinka concentration camp in 1942, wrote the following words:

'You say:
– "Dealings with children are tiresome".
You're right.
You say:
– "Because we have to lower ourselves to their intellect.
　Lower, stoop, bend, crouch down".

You are mistaken.
It isn't that which is so tiring. But because we have to reach up to their feelings. Reach up, stretch, stand on our tip-toes. As not to offend.'

If we impose other agendas upon our children, if we structure their lives so that the play agenda disappears entirely, the least we can expect from them is frustration and anxiety. A backlog of unresolved feelings will accumulate. Play helps children to explore and organize their feelings in a context which they can manage. Children do display a great need to replay the things that worry them. Play is not only an outlet for exuberance but is also a medium for dealing with emotional conflict and uncertainties about the world. Children's play can become a metaphor for their feelings.

Playing at Divorce, Birth, Marriage, Death – the determining moments in any individual's life – is essential. Children need to, and do, *think* about things through the medium of their play. How else can they express their grief, their joy? Children's thinking is not head-bound but is enacted in the willed landscapes of their play. Problems are played out in order to be understood. A play scene can settle turbulent feelings; deal with loss; make sense of confusion, and reorder the world for the child. Denial of this experience creates deep resentment. Play is 'thinking/feeling time' to a child in need. To be directed to play to an outer goal may constitute an emotional infringement against the child. As Margaret Lowenfeld has written,

'This necessity of the human mind to dramatise these elements of its environment that it perceives, in order to be able to emotionally assimilate them, is a characteristic that runs throughout the whole fabric of human life.'[41]

A modern adaptation of a ring game, similar to that described in the previous chapter, reflects today's insecurities. The marriage game 'Poor Jenny is a-weeping' now has an extra verse. Jenny, a sad girl, weeps firstly for her sweetheart, then, in turn, for her bridesmaids, pageboys, vicar, and a church. Eventually, her heart's desires are met, the weeping stops and she marries. In the last verse of the original song, Jenny dances with her husband on her wedding day. In the new version, there is an almost imperceptible pause and then Jenny starts weeping again. The refrain now goes: 'Poor Jenny is divorcing…'. As a postscript to that sad little tale, Jenny often re-marries, so a happy ending is possible – alternatively, she might even learn to enjoy being single.

A woman whose father's recurrent illness was re-created in her play is quoted by Singer and Singer.[42] Her imaginary characters included Phena and Barbara Tall, as well as Ultra, Violet, and Ray. These pharmaceutical characters were often worked into a game-show quiz.

Many parents worry about their child's imaginary companions, but they have been positively correlated with less aggression in boys, greater happiness, more positive attitudes, less fear and anxiety during later play situations, and greater persistence in play. Girls with play companions were less prone to anger, fearfulness, and particularly sadness in their play.[43]

One man I met developed his own little world, or paracosm, over 40 years ago, and wrote to me about his childhood game. His name was Richardson, and when times were tough, he would call on his gang for help. Out of the wall they would come, 'a hierarchy of fellows': Semner and Demner and possibly Memnor and Temnor, led by the central character, the boy himself, splendidly titled: 'The Richardson dipped in Gravy'. When alone in his bedroom he would enact, or rather 'become', these characters. In his words: 'The characters were always involved in some heroic deeds against some injustices, defending the honour of some damsel in distress. There was many a rough and tumble on the bed between the Richardson D.I.G. and his men and the baddies. The greater the threat to the Richardson, the more "disciples" were called upon. It is possible my Teddy Bear, Peter, got caught up in this too.'

As a postscript, he added that, apart from his mum and dad, he didn't think he had shared this with anyone before. In conclusion, Richardson, man and child, agreed: 'I'm happy for you to use this in any research material or book or whatever. (The Richardson nods his approval.)'

Too much directed play, with predetermined outcomes and learning objectives, will lead to frustration and unhappiness because what the child wants to explore through play will remain problematic. Unfortunately, much play in schools functions in this way, prioritizing only the intellectual/skill aspect of human nature and neglecting the affective side. This is demonstrably counterproductive, as a frustrated or unhappy child will have more difficulty in learning.

Spontaneous play, with adult interventions only when necessary, allows the development of an *integrated personality.* Respecting what Piaget describes as 'compensatory play' – in which a child replays events which may have been difficult or challenging – acknowledges the child's right to feel and express sad or happy moods. As a mother, I spent far too much time trying to cheer my children up, probably for my own benefit. I wanted happy children, and didn't appreciate their need sometimes to feel sad. Sad play can eventually help to promote well-being.

Play is invaluable where a child is anxious or worried. Good hospitals know this, and have successfully used play therapy for a number of years. (See Russell Evans's book *Helping Children to Overcome Fear.*[44]) Research shows that children who play at hospitals – with doctors, operations, bandages, etc. – show less resistance to medical procedures and recover more swiftly.

'Adults reflect through discussion, through literature, through writing and meditation. Children reflect through concretely acting out past experiences, or concretely preparing for them.'

Tina Bruce[45]

In my time as a kindergarten teacher, I witnessed many little girls, and fewer boys, playing sick babies. Boys preferred to be dogs with wounded paws. Death and loss were intermittently recurring themes – as they are in life. The following anecdotes are examples of the importance of children's feelings and of the need, at times, to prioritize them over other educational outcomes.

During the inspection of a particular kindergarten the children had behaved in an exemplary fashion and were beginning to get the hang of what it was their unusually inquisitive visitor wanted from them. On a walk across a field the inspector asked a spirited boy how many sheep he could see. Bemused at the question, the answer to which he knew was obvious to both of them, but now also canny about the way this inspection game worked, the boy responded: 'Two, but they have eight legs'. The inspector looked pleased and scribbled on her clipboard (evidence of arithmetical ability here). On their return, the same boy, eager to please, continued to inform her that his chair normally had four legs, six when he sat on it (ha!), but only two when he swung backwards. The world-view of this intelligent child was rapidly contracting into a never-ending vision of legs – all expertly tailored to fit the anticipated frame of the inspector's questions. Later, the teacher brought some sparkling frozen winter leaves inside, and in a mood of silent fascination and amazement, the children watched the delicately frosted tracery disappear as the leaves slowly thawed in the warmth of the room. When the session was over, the inspector informed the teacher that the observation of the leaves had been a 'very good science lesson', but that she was keen to know where exactly the children had recorded their experiences. The teacher put her hands to her chest and answered with the exasperated passion of one who has little expectation of being understood: 'In their souls'. The inspector dutifully recorded it on her pad....

At a conference at Newcastle University ('Realising Children's Potential', September 1997), counsellor and therapist Kathy Hunt gave a moving account of a small girl's overwhelming grief at losing her mother, who had died of cancer. The child needed to be held, would not tolerate change in the nursery, and was exhibiting 'all the identified behaviours associated with mourning – the panic, the crying out loud, searching in places over and over again. Wandering, unable to settle, very little ability to concentrate.' Slowly the child began to play. Hunt describes what happened.

> 'She began by selecting a plastic polar bear and its baby in the small world water play area of the nursery. She spent hours playing the same identically repeated game in the coloured-blue, cold water. Around the top of the water trough there was a small circular path. Sally would walk the adult and baby polar bear along the path circling the blue water. Every so often she would drop the baby into the water and let it sink to the bottom; then she would exclaim, with a deep intake of breath, 'Oh no!' – and with this the game would begin again.'

Hunt describes this play as a metaphorical process. The child, she said, '...has created a metaphor that expresses the meaning she intends. She needs to play this game in order to make sense of her experience.'[46]

Kathy Hunt sensed that she was driven to play and to repeat it, and that her own task was to respect and value this process by giving Sally the time, space, and privacy to play. Kathy was the important adult in this child's life who was able to sanction play. Eventually the little girl stopped. Her emotional readjustment had begun. The adults provided the room, the time, and the space but, I would suggest, it was *the genius of play* which led the child to find the right metaphor for her feelings, and so to move on.

Jane Hislam cautions against the view that children are always 'playing things out', in either a conditioned or therapeutic sense, although she also acknowledges that '...at some level children's play acts as a kind of personal mirror and that through play children are coming to grips with their own realities.'[47] When a child *has* exteriorized her inner reality in play– the better to get a clearer look at it – everyone else can see it too! Parents and teachers need sensitivity and respect when these open secrets are unwittingly shared.

Play embraces children's total experience. They use it to tell their stories; to be funny and silly; to challenge the world; to imitate it; to engage with it; to discover and understand it; and to be social. They also use play to explore their inmost feelings. In a single game – playing alone or with friends – the child can switch play modes, one minute imitating the television, the next making a discovery which leads to new thinking, then being reminded of something else and changing the play accordingly, and then suddenly being swamped by feelings, which require their own corresponding set of images, propelling the game in yet another direction. Like dreams, play is not ordered and rational. It does not give priority to one kind of experience or one kind of knowledge over another.

Rudolf Steiner likens playing to dreaming. In dreaming, he says, adults remain at play throughout their lives. Disconnected images from many levels of our experience rise up and fade away like great waves, sometimes leaving us with significant images and sometimes in total bewilderment. Like explorers, as image players we enter our dream world somehow to shift the events in our life, real and imagined, into a new shape – as children order and reorder their play. (Interestingly, dream-sleep deprivation results in hallucinatory experiences in waking life – indicating that dreaming [and play] are linked to well-being and mental stability.)

Playing out negative emotions can present a challenge to adults. There is no doubt that this kind of play is hard to handle. However, Margaret Lowenfeld[48] suggests that *unmet* 'emotional satisfactions' from childhood, including the forces of destruction, aggression, and hostility – which can be safely displayed through play and then integrated into the personality – reappear unconsciously in adult life as negative drives, which seek outlets in industrial competition, anarchy, and ultimately war. In her view, the pretend games of conflict in childhood, involving aspects of human behaviour such as destruction, aggression, and hostile emotion, which 'form so powerful an element for good or evil in the human character', function as a kind of safety valve against potentially dangerous adult drives.

I remember a boy in my kindergarten staging a kick-boxing tournament – to my mind an aggressive and dangerous sport. He set up a ring, invited the girls and the more timid boys to buy tickets (which he made) to watch the spectacle, and began touting for sparring partners. A 'contestant' was found, his best friend, and they began to play together using a repertoire of largely imitated aggressive gestures: scowling, posturing, air punching, boxer's toe dancing, and – yes – kicking. The protagonists went through the whole gamut of emotionally aggressive behaviour, and yet they were as gentle and controlled with each other, in their choreographed and mimed aggression, as two ballet dancers. I watched with bated breath, ready to intervene at any moment – a stance which, in the event, proved unnecessary. To claps and cheers, the winner received the vase of flowers sitting conveniently on a nearby window-sill grasped in an inspired move by his partner; the boxing ring became a circus and the audience joined in.

At other times the boys, and less often the girls, would be fierce dogs, complete with studded collars and leads. These dogs needed to be mastered. There was always an interesting dynamic between dog and master: if the dog was too aggressive and wayward on its lead, the game would fail as the master would be pulled about willy-nilly. It was an exercise in control: the master needed to learn how to master the dog, and the dog to be ruled by the master. We need both behaviours in self-management and self-restraint, and there are times in life, when we need to be ruled by the wisdom of others. (Playing at Kings and Queens and their subjects, especially when roles are interchangeable, is helpful in this sphere, as are games about parental/school discipline.)

Teachers learn that rough and tumble play is common and exists along a continuum commensurate with children's developmental ages.[49] I believe bullying, intimidation, and behaviour which really frightens or threatens other players is unacceptable. Pretend fear, however, is different and exciting. Following Lowenfeld, what I am arguing for is the understanding that a play context in which no one is hurt, and which stays at the level of fun, is a positive and enabling way of dealing with powerful feelings.

I also recognize that aggression, anger, and intimidation constitute a major part of some children's lives. For those children who live in constant fear, one would expect, at some level, to see it reflected in their play. If this is handled sensitively it can be the safest arena for dealing with emotions which, as Lowenfeld suggests, in a different sphere might otherwise become destructive. We need to be tolerant and understanding as well as protective when we see this happening. Sadly, we live in a society in which violence is commonplace – violence which our children cannot help but imitate. It is not the child's imitation which is at fault – the fault lies with society. The teacher/parent needs great skill and understanding to deal with its inevitable appearance in children's play.

Empathy

Daniel Goleman[50] believes that well adjusted adults are people who have 'self-awareness, zeal, and motivation'. They are empathic, socially deft, and can exert impulse control. A well adjusted adult is by definition an emotionally intelligent person. Quoting Martin Hoffman's research, Goleman describes the great capacity babies have to participate in the feelings of others through what he describes as 'motor mimicry'. Such a strong and immediate rapport do they have with others, he claims, that a baby hearing another child cry *will cry as if she herself were hurt.* There is an adjustment, an alignment with the other's feelings. A baby will put her own fingers in her mouth if she sees a baby with hurt fingers 'to see if she hurts too'. 'On seeing his mother cry, one baby wiped his own eyes, though they had no tears.'[51] Goleman again: 'Empathy stems from a sort of physical imitation of the distress of another, which then evokes the same feelings in oneself'.[52]

The Greeks felt that the experience of *mimesis* or imitation, especially in music, could arouse within the imitator ethical feelings of a positive or negative kind. Each of their musical modes had differing ethical significance, a different ethos. The Lydian mode, sadness; the flute, excitement.[53]

At about one year of age an infant will attempt to soothe another by offering a doll, or even her own mummy, to help. The older baby not only feels the other's pain reverberate in herself, but because of the intense experience of the other within, will also now try to find a more personal and appropriate solution to help. The altruistic nature of the human spirit in its germinal form is alive and well in the very earliest months of childhood.

Infant and childhood empathy create a foundation for later empathy, which leads to the ability to perceive the subjective experience of another person. Daniel Goleman argues that the empathic affect, the capacity for putting oneself in another's place, leads people to follow certain moral principles and to altruism. Living into the plight of the other can buttress moral convictions in adult life, and help us to be conscious of the need to alleviate misfortune or injustice against others. It also acts as a deterrent to prejudice and superficiality. In empathy play, through imitation, I put myself in your place – I play at being you.

A five-year-old girl in my kindergarten whose mother was working had spent some time being cared for by a woman with a new baby. One day she took one of the soft baby dolls, drew the curtains, made herself a cup of pretend tea and a biscuit (a conker), and sat down with her baby. She told everyone to ssshh! Then, she carefully placed her doll in one arm, lifted her jumper and began to breast-feed. So successful was her re-creation and so deep her absorption that a great peace descended on the room and the other children walked past her with care. Occasionally she lifted her small cup of tea and had a nibble of a biscuit – as nursing mothers do. In her imitation she had perfectly captured the qualities of a

nursing mother with her child. This small girl had moulded her own frame to the precise contours of another. The moral forces imitated in her play appeared in the cast of her body rather than in her conscious mind; as Goethe says, 'Love does not rule but shapes and that is more'.

Tina Bruce gives a touching example of a child who begins to explore, through unsentimental imitation, the very different thoughts, feelings, and experiences of someone else:

> 'A new girl called Jo joined a nursery class. Jo had an artificial arm and two girls, Nadia and Jody, were fascinated when she took it off at story time because she did not want to wear it all the time. That afternoon, the children played together and Nadia was Jo. Through her play, Nadia entered an alternative world to her own, in which she had no arms. She used all her knowledge of what arms are for and she came to know about Jo as she hadn't before.'[54]

In adults, this ability to enter an alternative world by 'empathizing' with someone else is the hallmark of a compassionate personality. Empathy play in childhood lays the foundation for this. What children do *physically* through their play, caring adults can later effect through the power of the imagination alone. A sympathetic listener often says: 'I can imagine how you must have felt – I wouldn't have liked to be in your shoes'.

Deep secrets are being revealed to the playing child through the initiations of the play ritual. Communion in its most pure and untutored form is being enacted, and intuition about the world of the other is at the centre of the ceremony. Like actors, children *re-create themselves in the mood of the other person*, reproducing every gesture, facial expression, tone of voice, effecting a 'magical transmission of emotion'.[55] If I imitate you consciously in my play, I also begin to understand you, to attune myself to you, to unite my being with yours. Fluttering through my empathy play is my fledgling love. ...

Everychild: Empathy

> 'Sometimes I'm afraid, sometimes I don't know what to do, I don't know what the script is, but let me be you, I want to know how you feel, think and act. I want to know what responsibility feels like, although I can't sustain it. I want to look through the looking glass into your world in the only way I can, through my play. How will it be to be you? Can I climb inside your skin, transform myself into you?'

'Human morality', says Rudolf Steiner, '...depends on the interest one man takes in another, upon the capability to see into the other man. ...Those who have the gift of understanding other human beings will receive from this understanding the impulses for a social life imbued with true morality'.[56]

Without empathy play, we may be doomed to live in a world lacking morality, looking only ever inwards. In her book *The Kindness of Children,* Vivian Gusin Paley makes a powerfully succinct statement about the importance of role-play:

> 'If the need to know how someone else feels is the rock upon which the moral universe depends, then the ancient sages were right. For this is surely what happens when children give each other roles to play in their continual inquiry into the nature of human connections. It is as schoolchildren that we begin life's investigations of those weighty matters.'[57]

Children sitting at desks doing work sheets or passively watching television are not engaging with these weighty matters. For young children to *do* is to understand, and in the case of role play: to do and to *be*. No swimmer ever learnt to swim from an instruction sheet or from watching others.

'You can be the big schoolgirl.' (How do big schoolgirls feel, act?)

'I'm a spaceship man.' (How might a spaceship man behave? What fears might he have? How might he face up to challenges?)

'This is the door of my kindergarten.' (Now I can be as kind or as unpleasant as my own teacher.)

'Are you a mouse?'

'No, I'm a prince.' (So you need to treat me very differently.)

'What can I be?' (Whatever you wish!)

The questions 'Who am I in this game?' and 'How must I be as my new self?' are major preoccupations for most young players. Through imaginative play, and in particular through sociodramatic play, children are able to express and explore their own viewpoints and feelings, and those of others.

In his book *The Development of Play*, David Cohen refers to the work of Tower and Singer (1980), who catalogued the many benefits of imaginative play. In addition to 'improved emotional well-being and self-control', 'self-entertainment reducing fear and anxiety', and 'poise', the social benefits of imagination included: 'becoming more sensitive to others' and 'increased empathy'. The researchers concluded that, 'the more a child imagines, the happier he, or she is.'[58] Empathic imitation in play helps counteract alienation and enhances social awareness. Living imaginatively into the experience of 'the other' awakens the ability to 'read' the thoughts and feelings of others, and the journey toward emotional and social literacy begins. Social imagination, which first appears in germinal form in the imaginative games of early childhood, is the kernel around which all mature and tolerant societies are formed.

It is my belief that by trusting to the wise tutelage of the spirit of play, we parents and educators can be partners in the creation of a social future, and that in the, 'Quick, now, here, now, always' of their play, children are learning nothing less than what it means to be human.[59]

Play and the Sense of Self

"Moon!" you cry suddenly, "Moon! Moon!"
The moon has stepped back like an artist gazing
amazed at a work
That points at him amazed.

Ted Hughes
'Full Moon and Little Frieda' (2 years old)[60]

Stuart Brown's work with animals led him to the belief that in spontaneous play something unique and individual is at work. Free from the laws of instinct and necessity, the genius of play, an independent spirit, nurtures in turn the spirit of those it inspires. To careful observers, a child's play reveals something of the innermost nature, both of the present child, and of the future self. Mysteries of the future are both hidden and revealed in the open secret of children's play.

Friedrich Froebel and Rudolf Steiner, both spirited and sensitive educators themselves, demonstrated a remarkable convergence of thinking on this point.

Froebel and Steiner on Play

'Play', said Froebel, '…is the highest expression of human development in childhood, for it alone is the free expression of what is in the child's soul. It is the purest and most spiritual product of the child and at the same time it is a type and copy of human life at all stages and in all relations… For to one who has insight into human nature, the trend of the future life of the child is revealed in his freely chosen play.' [61]

And Steiner tells us 'Form inner pictures of these children and then think quite hypothetically: the individual gesture as revealed in the child's play up to the second dentition will emerge again in the characteristic way in which, after the age of twenty, he will form personal judgements. In other words after their twentieth year, different people vary with regard to their personal judgement in the same way in which, as children, they have differed in their play before the change of teeth.' [62]

From Rudolf Steiner's description, one can visualize a child drawing toward herself certain toys and not others, selecting and structuring play opportunities specific to her need. Steiner links freedom in play and freedom in thought – pairing the child's ability to bring the right elements together to create her play with the way we cast around our mental landscape for arguments to support our judgements as adults. In adults the secret self works in private. In play the emergent self is revealed. Outer play becomes inner resource. The narrower the spectrum of choice, the more blinkered our thinking is likely to become. Playful adult thinkers are able to think 'out of the box': free-range players make free-range thinkers.

'What a human being acquires between birth and the change of teeth through the activity of playing, and what is enacted before our eyes in such a dreamlike manner, are the forces of the child's yet unborn spirituality.'

Rudolf Steiner[63]

Both Steiner and Froebel suggest that in the activities of *freely chosen play,* the child is telling us something about herself, about her own uniqueness. A playful prophet, she sits amongst her playthings – miniature auguries of her future – assembling the components of her intimated inner world.

It would be wrong to suggest that all play is either prognosis of the future or diagnosis of the past, but a wise eye may look for significances here and there, for glimpses of things that have been and might yet be. Anyone watching the play of the three sisters in the following story would not have been surprised at the future destinies of the girls.

As a child, the oldest sister loved to play 'Shops' – arranging and re-arranging small oddments for sale. The second sister played 'Schools' – giving expert instruction in the three Rs to all available dolls and siblings – willing or otherwise. The third sister played 'Nurse' to every needy being, including her devoted dog Mick who happily submitted himself to her tender ministrations – regularly sporting beautifully bandaged paws and suitably sad expression. In adult life, the three sisters became a shop-manager, a headmistress, and a hospital theatre-sister respectively.

These girls were indeed partners with their futures in their play.

Self and the World

Through imitation, reflection, and self-determined action, we gradually learn to know ourselves: as individuals with a rich inner life (world in me) and as participating, creative world beings (myself in the world). 'Making the inner outer and the outer inner' was axiomatic to the educational philosophies of Pestalozzi and Froebel.[64] It was also central to Rudolf Steiner.

The task of finding ourselves in the world, and the world in us, extends well beyond the confines of the narrow classroom, as

Seamus Heaney illustrates so brilliantly in his poem 'Personal Helicon'. Heaney keenly recaptures the boyhood experience of peering into a dark well and seeing his own white face reflected back at him from the watery depths below. The child poet calling down the 'dark drop' of the well hears the echo of his voice which '…gave back your own call / With a clean new music in it'. Each interchange, each 'call' and 'answer' to and from the world, brings about a delicate unfolding of a new self.

In a wonderful inversion Heaney links the vivid self-knowing of the engaged, playful, exploring, risk-taking child with the more distant self-knowledge of the rhyming, literate adult:

> *Now, to pry into roots, to finger slime,*
> *To stare big-eyed Narcissus, into some spring*
> *Is beneath all adult dignity. I rhyme*
> *To see myself, to set the darkness echoing.*
>
> Seamus Heaney, 'Opened Ground'[65]

Children today still need the peace of a long, slow-paced, active, and *engaged* childhood, with plenty of time to 'finger slime', peer into water, and make hosts of new discoveries which consolidate the process of knowing self and the world. As Joseph Chilton Pearce, former humanities teacher and author of *The Magical Child,* puts it:

'Structuring knowledge of the world takes at least six years because the world is filled with many things and its processes and principles are strict. The child is programmed to interact with the actual world: a place of rocks, trees, grass, bugs, sun, moon, wind, clouds, rain, snow, and a million things.'[66]

Play is the perfect bridge between self and the world of nature and the world of others. *I know myself in relation to what is outside me.*

Sociodramatic play is not only important for social development; it also promotes *self*-development. Herbert Mead (1863-1931) argued that children only develop a sense of self through role playing at being the other. In the words of Meltzner,

> 'In referring to the human being as having a self, Mead simply means such an individual may act socially towards himself, just as towards others. He may praise, blame or encourage himself; he may become disgusted with himself, may seek to punish himself, and so forth. Thus the human being may become the object of his own actions. The self is formed in the same way as other objects – through the definitions of others.'[67]

Thus begins the development of consciousness and conscience. I know who I am through my social interactions with others, and through regarding myself also as 'an other'. By recognizing the other as a coherent self-entity, I also come to know myself as a self. And by adjusting to others' perceptions of me I understand myself further. By being Robin Hood, Princess Crystal, the wicked witch, the giant, the rabbit, the lion, I also know myself when I am me again. Me, is one of the people I am.

'We need to make it clear that today's main paradigm for understanding a human life, the interplay of genetics and environment, omits something essential – the particularity you feel to be you. By accepting the idea that I am the effect of a subtle buffeting between heredity and societal forces, I reduce myself to a result.'

James Hillman[68]

James Hillman suggests that each life is formed by an image, an essence of life, which calls it to a destiny. This destiny is uniquely mine; it is distinct from my chromosomes or what my parents did or didn't do – it calls me to act. The call of that destiny is first heard in childhood. Our play helps us to reclaim the self. In our play, we assert our own-ness, follow our lodestar, and meet our essence.

> 'When my cousin and I took our porridge of a morning, we had a device to enliven the course of the meal. He ate his with sugar, and explained it to be a country continually buried under snow. I took mine with milk and explained it to be a country suffering gradual inundation. You can imagine us exchanging bulletins; how here there was an island still unsubmerged, here a valley not yet covered with snow; what inventions were made; how his populations lived in cabins on perches and travelled on stilts, and how mine was always in boats; how the interest grew furious, as the last corner of safe ground was cut off on all sides and grew smaller every moment; and how... the food was of altogether secondary importance, and might have been nauseous, so long as we seasoned it with these dreams.'
>
> Robert Louis Stevenson[69]

The wonderful milk-lapped treasure islands, spied by the eye of Stevenson's imagination in the breakfast bowl before him, have a unique quality, which prefigures what later appeared so vividly in the dramatic themes created by his literary genius. His play echoed the call of his destiny. The imagination, which – as in Stevenson's case – makes its first forays in the musings of childhood, is the subject of the next chapter.

4. The Truth of the Imagination

> 'I know of nothing but the holiness of the Heart's affections and the Truth of the Imagination.'
>
> John Keats[70]

My intention in this chapter is to plead for the 'Truth of the Imagination,' to borrow Keats's fine words.

Rationality works with the known, the finite. Imagination, on the other hand, is timeless and engages with the possibility of what might be. Imagination penetrates the veil of the future, and trawls the past to supply the human psyche with the multiplicity of meanings it needs; it lends wisdom to the soul. The mind's eye is the blind eye that also sees. It is the imagination of spring which helps us through the dark days of winter; the vision of spring's return, which allows winter's privations to be borne. Inner vision draws us on, giving us staying power and furnishing us with the necessary courage to win through against adversity. In troubled times our imagination, unbounded by time or place, reminds us that things will not always be as they are.

Like Keats, Wordsworth was an apologist for the imagination. His dazzling host of daffodils, probably first witnessed by the poet's sister Dorothy in the spring of 1807, still possess the power and immediacy to burst in upon me with their timeless glory. Swaying and tossing their golden heads in the breezy sunlight, they light my inward eye and defy the dullest day's weather. I first learnt that poem as a child; I am older and changed, but those dancing images have remained faithful and true, against the contingencies of my life. There is a constancy of the imagination. Poetic imagery heals our spirit and lifts our souls.

Imagination moves things along; it can give us lasting hope. It crosses boundaries, which we are unable to traverse physically. Charles Dickens wrote: 'Little Red Riding Hood was my first love. I felt that if I could have married little Red Riding Hood, I should have known perfect bliss.'[71]

Dickens effected huge social change through his writings. He possessed remarkable social imagination, could 'see' into the lives of others, and was able to write of their hardship, trouble and joy, with great clarity and feeling. That he should have had such longing in his childhood – his tender young self inspired by something that could never be and yet also might yet have been – is a poignant revelation about the wish and dream world of boy and man. In the crossing of the two worlds, all of us can begin to dance with our dreams.

'The concept of "what might be" – being able to move in perception from the concrete given, or "what is", to "what was, what could have been, what one can try for, what might happen" and, ultimately, to the purest realms of fantasy – is a touchstone of that miracle of human experience, the imagination.'

Singer and Singer[72]

Our imagination fires our will forces and we act to change the world. In play, children are also practising changing the world.

Combining something seen with the senses, with the imagination of a new context, they change their world – just as they see adults do around them.

Some boys in an indoor up-turned table-boat needed a radar. A black metal music stand was spied and instantly appropriated to function as a sky scanner in a new and imaginative setting. Few men and no women have set foot on the moon, yet thousands and millions of children have been there, in a variety of self-assembled play spacecraft, or in invisible flights of swift and soaring imagination.

The children in these photographs are making a creation with clothes-horses, string, wool, and cloths. In the recurring 'schemas' or 'muses', which regularly appear in children's games, the mirror of their physical play reflects not only their imaginations and

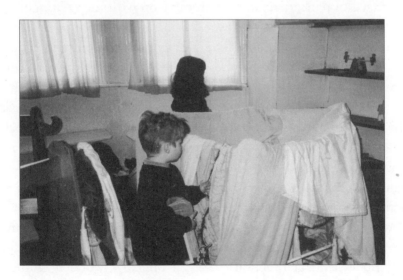

preoccupations but also the development of their mental/ physio-
logical processes. For example, when a child first begins to inwardly
experience the connectedness of his, or her, own developing
thoughts, a corresponding flurry of spontaneous, 'tying-things-

together' activity frequently appears in their play. (The use of logic in language, where one concept becomes *tied* to another in increasingly complex ways, is another sign that a child has reached this particular developmental stage.). The children pictured here are tying lengths of wool and string to represent 'electricity' – itself a medium and metaphor for a type of 'connectedness'.

Like many children, this group plays technical games fairly often, perhaps to gain mastery over things they do not understand. This spaceship had connecting 'wires for the electricity', with pegs hanging on the ends of the strings like jump-leads. The electrical circuits were laid down first. The wires were then covered over with cloths as cladding, so that they were no longer visible. One of the boys got an electric shock and died. After crying pitifully, 'I'm dead now' and resting for a while, he managed to reincarnate in time to carry on with the exciting play. The wires (wool and string) were deliberately chosen in different colours – yellow and red (live). One boy announced, 'These sparkly wires are extra powerful and they will get us to the moon'. I have no doubt they did.

It is worth noting that this spontaneous play meets and exceeds the requirements of what the current UK Early Learning Goals describe as 'Knowledge and Understanding of the World'. *Electricity* – its power, danger, and interconnectedness; *building* – substructure before superstructure, wires before walls. *Co-operation* – shared and agreed imaginations help when creating communally; *flexibility* – new ideas were incorporated into the plan, refining and improving it. *Symbolism* – wool/string as wire, different colours standing for different electrical functions, as in a plug. (A wooden clothes-horse is, incidentally, a wonderfully symbolic thing in itself – a metaphorical horse for clothes, like saddles, to be slung over.) *Aesthetics* – it had to look right. The game needed considerable technical expertise, and required fine motor skills, each piece of wool needing careful tying around the clothes horses.

The spaceship will not have been the only thing sparking, however. The complex physical activity will have been firing the transmitters along the neural pathways of the children's brains. The exciting fantasy of their spaceship, the issue from the comet's tail of their imaginations, will also have showered the children with a plethora of 'learning outcomes'.

Play and imagination help us to live in two worlds at once – an enriching and lifegiving capacity.

An education which neglects the imagination, which fails to acknowledge the child's vision and need for a life of the imagination, is one which stunts inner growth, and brings about a kind of soul poverty.

Parents know the value of imagination in making reality more bearable. A mother's lips weave a 'play magic' when they kiss a sore place better, and the pain is lessened because her magic works. A spoonful of medicine is bearable when it journeys to the mouth, sweetened by the images of a helicopter whirring through the skies on its way to a little red hangar waiting below. Climbing the stairs to bed is made easier when you can delight in the imagery of the phrase 'Up the wooden hill to Bedfordshire'.

The Intangibles

James Hillman believes that the imagination and the world of the intangible and the invisible are essential to human life. We need beauty, a sense of the invisible, and a connection with myth, which, in the words of the Roman philosopher Sallust, 'never happened but always is', Hillman says.[73] He maintains that we all need to feel a sense that life is invisibly backed – whatever our spiritual beliefs. We need a bridge to the invisible, and when the two worlds – the world of the visible and the invisible – part, there is insufferable desolation. When the visible world no longer sustains life, then humans, nature, and things become savage and hostile – the world tears us apart. Tribal societies are robbed of their spirits in exchange for goods; the most 'pathologized' moment in the entire incarnation story is the cry on the cross, which tells of the agony when one is encompassed only by the visible world.'[74]

'The great task of a life sustaining culture, then, is to keep the invisibles attached, the gods smiling and pleased: to invite them to remain by propitiations and rituals; by singing and dancing, smudging and chanting; by anniversaries and remembrances; by great doctrines such as the Incarnation and little intuitive gestures – such as touching wood or by fingering beads, a rabbit's foot, a shark's tooth; or by putting a mezuzah on the door-post, dice on the dashboard; or by quietly laying a flower on a polished stone.'

James Hillman[75]

The photograph shows the creation of a five-year-old girl, who played quietly and with absorption for about 30 minutes. I watched as she carefully laid her cardigan on some tree roots and began searching for leaves and flowers to place upon it. Each leaf was chosen with great care, as was the flower that then decorated it. Out of her cardigan she had, without instruction, made a small altar – a deeply satisfying experience which lifted the everyday to a new level; it honoured nature and nature's elemental beings. It invited the invisibles to stay attached. It made her happy.

Wonderfully resourceful in seeking out what they need for their own secret purposes children sometimes achieve this in the unlikeliest of ways. The now grown-up child who describes her dolls in Chapter 7, told me the following story about angels.

As a child, one of the places she had loved to visit was the local cemetery. She remembered running along, stick in hand, ready to clang the line of hanging watering cans. At her touch, like battered old birds swinging on their perches, each would rock on its hook and offer up its apology for a note.

The oblong plots were filled with cold, glittering, green stones, which mesmerized her. She would trickle the gems through her small warm fingers, making them grate together satisfyingly. She was endlessly enchanted with their bright noise and powder-dusted, emerald beauty.

Her deepest reverence, however, was reserved for the angels. Certain grave-stones were headed by graceful, stone angels. Beautiful beings, with serene faces, mighty wings and attitudes of devotion, these angels were utterly compelling to the small child. She loved these potent symbols of that other world where 'glory rules and light reigns,' with a passion. If only she could have one for herself!

On one of her visits – just as if it were meant to be – a fallen (though uncorrupted) angel lay before her on the ground. Poor angel! It obviously needed looking after. Small enough to fit into her pram, it was speedily covered by a blanket and whisked home, the heavy pram thudding and shaking its way over the uneven road – an unceremonious and hasty journey. Once home, the angel was taken into the front room, a room only ever used for 'best', and put on the windowsill. The little girl visited this room often, her heart overflowing with love and reverence.

At this point, the question of ownership had not yet arisen. However, before long, other 'dolls with wings' began to materialize. Graced by their presence, the narrow front room windowsill soon became home to a whole host of divine stone angels. The girl had discovered that a little discreet wobbling proved an effective way of liberating other angels from their posts in the cemetery, and each new angel was spirited home, via the trundling pram, to join the growing throng. The room, with its curtains closed, became the little girl's private sanctuary.

Her parents and grandparents were worried. 'I'd had a smack', she said, 'but I couldn't stop doing it. Oh, I loved those angels!' Eventually, the local policeman called round to talk to Gran. 'We've been watching her and we know what she's been doing. What are we going to do about it?', he asked. Gran acknowledged the problem and said that the family was at its wit's end with the child. Eventually it was decided that the angels should be returned. A few days later, Mum, Gran, and a rather down-hearted little girl duly set out on a mission to replace the beloved angels. 'There was a sea of angels', she said, 'I was so sad to see them go... How I loved them.'

Her need for these symbols of otherworldliness was overwhelming – more powerful than worldly scruples or adult constraints. The phase passed, of course, and she never 'borrowed' anything in this way again. Aside from the issue of taking 'what is not rightfully yours', it seems to me that the loan of these angels fulfilled, for a time, a great need in this child's heart. Through her angels, she found it possible to make a connection to the invisible. Their presence lifted her from the humdrum of the everyday into quite other realms of experience.

Humans have always looked to ritual and symbol as gateways to the spirit, and this young girl was no exception. She needed to create a particular experience for herself from what was available in her environment. To me, her childhood 'theft', though conventionally wrong, has something rather magnificent about it.

Imagine, for a moment, the intensity of her experience, as she stood alone in that small front room in the presence of at least seven stone angels. Imagine, and perhaps admire!

Children, far more than adults, are alive to what William James describes as 'the authentic tidings of invisible things'[76] – they are in tune with maintaining a connection with the invisible, with the unseen forces behind Nature, and the metaphysical world.

A colleague told me that his little three-year-old daughter was once playing in the garden, talking to – as she later told him – a fairy or a nature being. Watching her, what impressed him was that she would first speak animatedly to her invisible companion, then sit still for some time attentively *listening to the reply* – 'the invisibles', he felt, were not only attached, but actively communicating. Singer and Singer write:

> 'If a significant proportion of the adult world continues to hold an active belief in invisible spirits, let us not be surprised at our children's creation of make-believe friends or societies. In the past, when we have written or talked to groups about some of our own research on children's invisible friends, we have occasionally received letters from apparently socially adjusted people, including teachers, who claim that children, because of their innocence and freedom from adult guilt or complexes, are directly in touch with the invisible spirit world. Their 'imaginary' friends, these people write, are not make-believe at all.'[77]

I remember the end of a wonderful day on the Clent Hills in Worcestershire. My children, then aged six and four, had enjoyed the high, far-reaching views and the sight of the fiery sun sinking slowly and majestically behind the darkening hill. As we turned around to head for home my younger son ran back to the crest of the hill and bent down. I couldn't see what he was doing, and when he returned I asked him what had happened. 'I was just leaving some Smarties for the sun', he said. He had carefully placed a few of his precious sweets on the ground and made a tiny circlet of Smarties in the dampening grass.

I was with the same son, now aged 22, at the recent solar eclipse. The loss of the sun for just those few moments had a profound and moving experience on everyone present, and in my mind's eye another image slowly came to light – in the darkness I saw once again the sun sinking behind the ridge of the hill and the silhouette of a small child bending down to make his humble offering to the gods, by way of a 'thank you'. Hillman again:

> 'All this has nothing to do with belief and so it also has nothing to do with superstition. It's merely a matter of not forgetting that the invisibles can go away, leaving you with nothing but human relationships to cover your back. As the Greeks said of their gods: They ask for little, just that they not be forgotten.'[78]

Story and Myth

> 'If a child is told only stories "true to reality" (which means false to important parts of his inner reality), then he may conclude that much of his inner reality is unacceptable to his parents. Many a child thus estranges himself from his inner life and this depletes him. As a consequence he may later, as an adolescent, no longer under the emotional sway of his parents, come to hate the rational world and escape entirely

into a fantasy world, as if to make up for what was lost in childhood.'

Bruno Bettelheim[79]

In her book *Assessing Children's Learning,* Mary Jane Drummond refers to Kieran Egan's work on rationality, reality, and fantasy. She includes wonderful play examples in support of Egan's 'curriculum of the imagination'. In the examples, wolves, children, smurfs, and dragons have the most exciting and dramatic time together. Why, puzzles Egan, do children find these kinds of games more intellectually engaging and meaningful than the real world of the everyday? 'His conclusion', she writes, 'is that this way of framing the question is based on an improper distinction. Smurfs and wolves may not be part of everyday reality, but what they represent *is* intensely real, since, in children's play, wolves and smurfs and dragons stand for the unrelenting conflicts between the good and the bad, the big and the little, the brave and the cowardly, the oppressors and the oppressed... the embodiment of struggles between security and fear, love and hate'.[80]

Imaginative play can be exciting and playful and intensely serious. Egan's conclusion is that it is full of important content which is rich in meaning for children.[81]

Most stories and myths summon pictures of our frailties and strengths; of our lack of courage, our untamed desires, our way of putting self-interest above stewardship and also of our trials in overcoming obstacles. They acknowledge the highs and lows of the human condition in picture form. They can be a kind of guidebook to the inner life. When the picture of the human being is put before the child, something of her own nature and that of others is revealed.

Good fairy stories and myths, although not strictly 'true' – at least to the rational mind – offer a message, a line of thinking, and most importantly, a *moral imagination* to our inner selves. The brothers Grimm speak of 'the fairy tale tutorial, for the spiritual welfare of the individual and the community'. Stories, myths, and imaginary play teach us truths about the world.

There is an old Jewish tale which goes like this:

'Fairy Tale and Truth went together for a long journey. One day Truth said to Fairy Tale: "How come, whenever we are seen together, people receive you with open arms and leave me outside? What could we do about this?" At that moment Fairy Tale gave its clothes to Truth. And from that day on Truth walks on earth dressed in the clothes of Fairy Tale.'[82]

The story of 'The Seven Ravens'

I once told the story of 'The Seven Ravens' to my five- and six-year-old kindergarten children. In this story, a little girl must rescue her seven brothers, who have been turned into ravens. The morning star gives her a small chicken bone to open the glass mountain within which her brothers are imprisoned. Unfortunately she loses the star's present and the only thing she can do is cut off her own little finger to use as a key to open the door. Through this sacrifice, she manages to rescue her brothers, who embrace and kiss her, and together they go home. When I told this story, one little girl was particularly affected. She was always beautifully dressed, like a little doll – as pretty as a picture – always perfectly turned out. 'Sally', she said, in consternation, 'did she have to cut off her finger, couldn't she do anything else?'. 'No', I answered, 'that really was the only thing she could do'. The moral dilemma elegantly presented in the fairy tale had given her cause for thought. For her the fairy tale tutorial played around the idea that the reach of goodness can extend beyond the measure of physical perfection.

Bruno Bettelheim, author of *The Uses of Enchantment: The Meaning and Importance of Fairy Tales,* quotes the writer G. K. Chesterton, whose belief in fairy tales was steadfast and sustaining, and who wrote:

> 'There is the lesson in Cinderella which is the same as that of the Magnificat – *exaltavit humiles* (He lifted up the humble). There is the great lesson of 'Beauty and the Beast', that a thing must be loved before it is loveable.'[83]

'Fairy' stories paint pictures of our human feelings, of our courage and frailties – as personified by the greedy wolf, the honest miller's son, the courageous youngest prince, the loyal daughter; they also tell of trickery, treachery, cruelty, and folly. Stories give an overview of life: all situations of human experience are within the wisdom of fairy tales, and the story is always for *us*. All the characters in one story make up a whole because all qualities, good and bad (and everything in between), are an essential part of human nature. The nastiness of the witch and the nobility of the king are (potential) aspects of my own being. Who am *I* in this story? Did *I* share my bread with the little old man? Or did I walk on unmoved? This is the realm of heroes, heroines, and villains. What lives in our souls can help us to overcome our shortcomings, and sometimes to rise above ourselves. A world which is totally rational and truthful is not necessarily the world of our total experience as human beings; and stories and myths can play a huge part in shaping not only what is, but also what might be, in the education of our ethical selves – not only who we are but also who we might become.

Egan labels the early years 'The Mythic Phase', a time when children are concerned with big issues – love, hate, jealousy – which are the ways in which they first understand the world. They learn to know the world, he suggests, through bipolar opposites such as good/evil, diligent/lazy, cruel/kind. He also says that children are not best served by sentimental or trivial stories:

> 'Programmed reading schemes, and the absence of powerful emotional, dramatic, and intellectual content… typify many primary classrooms… Disney-esque sentimentality is the exact emotional equivalent of intellectual contempt.'[84]

Egan's claims are reassuring for those of us who are alarmed at some of the dramatic and powerful play we might witness.

In a London kindergarten, a six-year-old girl was playing very tenderly with a rocking horse: she put a woven shopping bag around its head, where it hung from its ears, a swaying nose-bag full of delicious 'oats'. Suddenly she swung away and said loudly, 'I eat elephants, slugs, and snakes. I have a big mouth. I eat in one big gulp because I'm a witch. I'm half eagle, half human, because I've got an eagle heart.' Then she said to a friend, who, I should add, was utterly unfazed by her request, 'Do you mind if I do an operation to take out your heart as my biscuit and your blood as my tea?'. 'Actually I eat myself and then I come again.' 'I once was a girl' [performs a spell]… 'Oh no, I'm a crocodile now', [slithering to the ground]; 'I'll go and live with the crocodiles now.'

Her Promethean-like play has all the qualities of a good myth. 'Heart biscuits' and 'blood tea' are interesting – with echoes of other deeply symbolic rituals. The oral, mythic mind can live in this realm with impunity, and return to reality in an instant – as we might do after watching a Greek tragedy. In the Edda, the origin of the world, the primordial giant Ymir is killed by the gods: the earth is made from his flesh, the seas and lakes from his blood, the mountains from his bones, the trees from his hair, the sky from his skull.[85]

Possibilities of Being

This is the creature there never has been.
They never knew it, and yet, none the less,
they loved the way it moved, its suppleness,
its neck, its very gaze, mild and serene.
Not there, because they loved it, it behaved
as though it were. They always left some space.
And in that clear unpeopled space they saved
it lightly rested its head, with scarce a trace
of not being there. They fed it, not with corn,
but only with the possibility
of being. And that was able to confer
such strength, its brow put forth a horn. One horn.
Whitely it stole up to a maid – to be
within the silver mirror and in her.

Rainer Maria Rilke, 'The Sonnets to Orpheus'[86]

The realm of the subjunctive – the kingdom of our wishes, hopes, fears, imaginings, and possibilities – is also our real world.

One boy in my kindergarten had experienced tremendous physical problems. He had Talipes and had spent much time either in hospital or in recovery. I remember his profound bravery, and absolute lack of self-pity. One day he and a friend chose to play a game in which they were animals. His totemic play creature was a cheetah. His father pointed out that the cheetah was the fastest creature on earth and his son the slowest person in kindergarten. Through his chosen play emblem, the child could transcend his physical limitations, achieve his greatest desire, run like the wind, and become a free spirit.

The play curriculum is wonderfully democratic and inclusive.

To deny the imagination ill-equips the child for life's complex demands, as Joseph Chilton Pearce illustrates in his inspiringly titled book *The Magical Child*. He relates the story of a distressed nine-year-old boy who had been brought to the therapist Frances Wickes. His scrupulously honest parents had not wanted him to be saddled with 'the wealth of silly nonsense that seems to plague most children'; consequently, his childhood had been devoid of fairies, angels, Christmas beings, and imaginative stories. His well-meaning, rational parents had always told him 'the truth' about world events. Birth, for example, had been explained in full technicolour detail, complete with pictures and diagrams. As a result, he had became a precociously intelligent, sober, and articulate child. At around seven, however, there began to be problems. He couldn't be separated from his parents; he had serious night terrors, began to wet the bed, and grew thin and frail. Wickes 'took her cue from the child' and advised the parents to tap into the child's need for fantasy. The child needs:

> '…hours and hours a day of nothing but fantasies, fairy tales, wild imaginative stories', she said. 'Throw in all the talking animals, cloud castles, little people, magic and mystery, signs and miracles, Santa Claus and angels, fairy godmothers and wonderful wizards. Saturate him with the unreal and improbable. Make up stories for him, and enter into fantasies with him. Talk to the flowers with him, converse with the trees and wind, animate every nook and cranny of his life with imaginary beings.'[87]

Before long, the child was well again and back at school. The world was too much with this little boy. In knowing, categorizing, and rationalizing, his imagination had been laid waste.

The ability to imagine beyond what is perceptible to the senses saves us from the stifling grip of an overly rational world.

As mentioned on page 43, our psyches demand that we dream a little. People deprived of dream sleep, although not tired because they have slept deeply, begin to hallucinate during the day. To be whole and well we *need* our visions, it seems. Toward the end of his life Albert Einstein said that he valued the gift of his fantasy above all his abilities in abstract intellectual reasoning. Our imagination gives us joy and courage; it lets us try out things with impunity; it surprises and occasionally frightens us. Imagination is the bridge to intuition – to the *ahah!* moment – and is sometimes the direct route to inspiration.

The exercising of the imagination is a pleasurable experience for adults and children alike. Music, art, and poetry require the subtle alchemy of imagination to transform the commonplace into the arresting. Much of what we see and hear around us is the result of imaginations being made visible. Each performance of Shakespeare is different because different imaginations have been woven into the directing and acting of the particular performance. Inner pictures flow into outer creations. An actor without imagination – with no inner life – is shallow and unbelievable; paradoxically, we need the actor's fantasy to sustain our own belief.

I once asked my own son whether he wanted a bedtime story from a picture book or a made-up story, which I would tell rather than read him. His answer surprised me. He said, 'I want a coloured-in story, from your body!' For him, the pictures with colour were inside his own imagination. So often, our own images are superseded by the powerful visual representations of television and film. The film has a way of hijacking the individual imagination. Who has not lost something, some intimacy with the characters, when seeing the film of the book? How hard it is to retrieve our own images afterwards. Many children have been frightened by the wicked queen in Disney's 'Snow White' – their own pictures had not frightened them in the same way because they were created at *the child's own* manageable level of tolerance to fear. Researchers have noted a correlation between children's aggressive and anxious fantasies and the use of television.[88]

Most of our greatest thinkers also possess mighty imaginations. Einstein, who was a late reader, once said that the way to make children clever was to tell them fairy tales. To make them *really* clever, he said, tell them *lots* of fairy tales. The childhood imagination, the gift for fantasy, is easily gobbled up by the plethora of manufactured imaginations promulgated by television programmes, film, and advertising campaigns. The imagination is made a materialist – a hoarder of borrowed images. A truly awful world-view lurches into being, with all trains being Thomas, every lion a Lion king, all sharks Jaws, Cleopatra forever Elizabeth Taylor. Our 'ways of seeing' become bland, stereotyped, and fixed – or recurringly frightening. Research suggests that heavy TV viewers become lax at creating their own images when reading.[89] Here are Singer and Singer as before:

'For most people, the make-believe of childhood, with its elements of freedom from the constraints of physical structures and time or person-boundedness, lives on in the privacy of thought… The possession like quality of one's images, wishes, expectations, and beliefs becomes a closely guarded feature of one's sense of individuality and uniqueness.'[90]

The research scientist and the Professor of Psychology, Dorothy and Jerome Singer respectively, cite studies of the Kaiapo Indians in Brazil where a satellite dish has made television accessible. Labelled 'the big ghost' by the villagers, it has changed their community. No longer do they gather at night to chat, tell stories, share information. In the words of their oldest medicine man, Beptopup: 'The night is the time the old people teach the young people. Television has stolen the night.' As Singer and Singer wryly observe, for many in the United States, 'it has also stolen the day'. Television-viewing has become a way of life; in America, pre-school children watch up to 21 hours of television a week, and American families, on average, 28 hours per week.[91] Marie Winn, author of *The Plug-in Drug*, suggests that many American pre-schoolers may be watching up to a staggering *54 hours of television per week*.[92] A withering of the unique and individual imagination seems inevitable. Some six-year-olds, more accustomed to the visual image, were *told* a story recently. They were baffled. 'Where is the story?' they asked, 'we can't see it.'

Other Worlds

Like the boy described in Chapter 3, many children share the gift of creating coherent other worlds or 'Paracosms' in their play. David Cohen describes the Brontë children as having created a wonderful world called Gondal, which was peopled with dashing, military officers. They recognized its significance in their subsequent ability as adult writers to create character, plot, and narrative. Sometimes, Cohen suggests, these worlds can also be created to 'compensate for emotional absence and trauma' – to fill in the gaps, perhaps, supplying the child with what he or she lacks.[93]

'Imaginary playmates and paracosms may chiefly represent the vast creative potential of inherently talented people, but in less elaborated forms they may also represent what the childhood imagination can offer to the growing person. Humanity has already benefited from the paracosmic visions of Plato, Thomas Moore, Aldous Huxley....'

Singer and Singer[94]

In a small-scale study for the Institute of Steiner Waldorf Education, a group of students was asked to study children at their free play. Our objective was to find out what they were actually playing, and to classify some of the different types of play. One of the graduate students, Edward Marks, observed a group of twelve children at the Ringwood Waldorf kindergarten (UK). Although such studies are prone to subjectivity, Edward strove to be rigorous and respectful in his methods. He never interfered – not even to ask questions – as he felt that any involvement on his part would subtly affect and alter the play. He was also aware that children have a sure-fire instinct for knowing when they are being watched, so he occupied himself with some small task such as sewing, and made his notes discreetly. He aimed to be a friendly presence without disturbing the children. Creative playtime lasted for just over an hour and a half each morning, and over a period of 11 days Edward was able to observe almost 17 hours of un-interrupted play. During this time he recorded a total of 54 'themes' – all of which were initiated by the children. The teacher also intervened as little as possible – only making helpful suggestions or giving direction when it seemed absolutely necessary.

The following list is a selection of some of the themes:

horses and masters	cafe
cheese factory	big school
paper factory	insects
spaceship and dragon	fishing
really big house or castle	ferry boat
dark houses (with lantern)	doll as baby
car journey – as mice	wizard of dark house
cooking	home-made 'weeing' doll
ironing	having lots of visitors
trains and engines	shopping
forest	pussy cats
snakes (snake mummies, daddies, brothers & sisters etc.)	

'Kinderspiele' (Childrens' Games), Pieter Breugel, 1560

Hyderabad, India

Feeding time

Trains

Boats

Planes

Sand

Sand

Low structure materials

Low structure materials

Rough and tumble

Outside play

House cleaning

The themes flowed into one other, involving different groups of children at different times, and allowing inspirations for play to rise and fall in a kind of co-operative dream of the imagination. New belief systems were invented and willingly adopted in a process which Coleridge understood as 'That willing suspension of disbelief for the moment, which constitutes poetic faith'.[95]

In his studies of child cognitive development, Howard Gardener redefines intelligence into 'core components of multiple intelligences[96] which are: linguistic, logical-mathematical, bodily-kinesthetic, naturalist, musical, spatial, interpersonal, and intra-personal intelligence(s). He might also add imaginative intelligence to his list. So far, no computer has yet been programmed with its own imagination, nor has it invented anything new.

> 'Imagination means creating images that are not present to the senses. All of us exercise this faculty virtually every day and every night... the whole crux of human intelligence hinges on this ability of mind.
>
> ... nature has not programmed error into the genetic system and ...the child's preoccupation with fantasy and imagination is vital to development.'
>
> Joseph Chilton Pearce[97]

The use of the free imagination, and the possibility it gives for moving beyond the confines of a difficult situation, have also been a life-saving gift for those in captivity or in hiding, as Brian Keenan, John McCarthy, and many others have testified. Eisen's words speak for them all: 'With the aid of make-believe one could symbolically demolish the physical confines of a little room or bunker'[98] Imagining oneself in better conditions, in different relationships, powerful instead of helpless, gives hope in the face of suffering – the possibility of freedom again.

There is a link between play, the imagination, language development, and the arts. The budding forms of all artistic activity can be seen when children are at play. In the next chapter, I explore some tentative connections between play, language, and the arts.

5. Play, Language, and the Arts

In this ambitiously titled chapter, a subject which others have written about in far more detail, I hope to forge a few small but significant links between childhood play and the chain of experiences and expressions loosely labelled 'the arts'.

What children actually *do* when they play is a complex and fascinating issue. Lowenfeld, Drummond and others, have argued that part of what children represent in their play is an undifferentiated expression of what we later come to call art, literature, and drama. Children are in a state of perpetual metamorphosis and have the ability to move like quick-fire, from the fantastic to the everyday and back again, in a moment. The never-ending drama of 'their play' embraces all the arts in a kind of living tableau. They play as the spirit moves them: the same attendant spirit, I would suggest, which later inspires our creative outpourings as adults.

Mary Jane Drummond quotes Margaret Lowenfeld, the pioneering child psychotherapist, who identified a correlation between play and literature. Lowenfeld distinguished three types of imaginative play which correspond to 'three common attitudes in the creation of literature – Realism, Romance and Satire'. As Mary Jane Drummond explains:

> 'In realistic play, children represent the features of their daily lives as exactly as they can remember: this kind of play is well

known to educators, who provide many materials to support such play (pots, pans, kettles, ironing boards and so on). In romantic play, children create variations of the world in which they live, embodying secret longings of their own, "representing life not as it is but as they would like it to be" (Lowenfeld, 1935: 135). This kind of play, too, is commonly provided for – capes and crowns, fine robes and silver shoes are popular properties in the exercise of this kind of thinking and feeling. Lowenfeld's third category, satirical play, in which children satisfy their feelings by violent distortion of familiar themes, is less likely to be welcomed by educators...' [99]

In the Ringwood kindergarten study described in the previous chapter (page 78), the children usually named their games, as a way of defining their subject and of signalling the start of a particular play. Naming the game also allowed everyone entry to the same imaginative sphere. Roles were allocated, and characters defined and refined, as the action progressed. This process of definition was very important to them; like our literary use of titles, chapter headings, and character delineation, it helped the children to establish a framework of meaning for their play narrative.

Sometimes a theme would be played and then abandoned – to be revived again later that day or during the following days. Themes were played out in a variety of ways including socio-dramatic play; solitary play; exploratory play and play involving leaders and followers. Play would sometimes follow a 'script', as in one game where Peter Pan and Wendy made a brief appearance. The two arrived, delivered their set-piece speeches – important to the progress and direction of the game and helpful in confirming the leader's point of view – and then disappeared again. Re-enactment of puppet stories was common, and in these games narrative, dialogue, and set design would feature strongly. Puppets who fell over would be repositioned and ordered, by authorial command, to 'stay!' as children took responsibility for what should or should not happen in their stories.

'We're mischievous mousies, yeah?' was the title and opening chapter of one game. Later on, knowledge, such as what mousies eat and what threatens them, was added (cheese and cats!). Further chapters included mousies getting into a car (with symbolic basket for steering wheel); mousies going shopping to buy food, and – inevitably – mousies being chased by cats. As Singer and Singer write,

> 'One of the mysteries of human development involves the transformation of children's play from behaviour expressed in overt speech and action into one that flowers and expands privately through interior monologue, daydreaming and fantasy.'[100]

At a certain point, play can be perceived as going underground; external verbal play becomes inward, silent 'self-talk'. This interior monologue, Singer and Singer suggest, reappears later, in art, poetry, and theatre. The inspirations which flow into the creations of such childhood worlds come from the same rich vein which we later tap when we write stories or poems as older children and adults.

Story and Language

Telling and writing stories relies upon playfulness and good use of language. Traditionally the telling of folk tales marked the coming of night, and created in the mind a different rhythm – a time to put aside the work of the day and enter a different consciousness. The brothers Grimm collected their best stories from a woman who lived near Kassel. She told her stories with obvious delight, as Padraic Colum explains in his introduction to the Grimms' tales, quoting the Grimm brothers:

' "Her memory kept a firm grip on all the sagas. She herself knew that this gift was not granted to everyone, and that there were many who could remember nothing connectedly. She told her stories thoughtfully, accurately, with wonderful vividness and evidently had delight in doing it. First, she related them from beginning to end, and then, if required, repeated them more slowly, so that after some practice, it was perfectly easy to write from her dictation." Very likely, because they had to write, they laid stress upon the storyteller's verbal memory but what was also important for the listeners, and some felt the true gift of the teller, was "her perception of pattern, and her real accomplishment making it, the pattern, evident" '.[101]

The beautifully chosen words, well-constructed narratives, and deep underlying structures and patterns in the traditional tales provide a wonderful first introduction to literature. Literacy evolves from oral culture and children are very active listeners; stories stimulate inner dialogue and emphasize flow in speech. Later, speech can be lifted into clear thought and expression of feeling.

Well-written tales always remain fresh, like great paintings, which can be revisited time and time again. They also reappear in play and give children opportunities to play with language.

A three-year-old child in kindergarten demonstrated her ability to make meaning out of her morning story by creating a new context to try out the words and phrases she had heard earlier. Taking a little stand-up puppet doll, she began to retell the story. As she carefully moved her puppet, who represented the good girl in the story, she was heard to say, in a voice of great precision and emphasis, and not without dramatic flourish: '...She was **a paragon** of virtue...'

The words she spoke so clearly *belonged* to the good girl in the story; they defined her – she was the quintessence of goodness. The small story-teller has become conscious that goodness has degrees. Although she may not know the meaning of the individual words, her understanding comes from the context in which they were used when she first heard them, and is now affirmed as she uses them again herself.

Symbolic Play and Language

Children's symbolic play – a way of imaginative seeing – has been found to enhance language development. Language itself is a complex symbol system where, put very simply, one thing stands for another. A word stands in place of either an object, quality, activity, experience, and so on. In written language, the letters stand for the sounds that make up the words

Symbolic play is different to functional play. In functional play children use objects, such as a small-scale dustpan and brush, in the way they have seen them used, i.e. for sweeping. The object fulfils the same function in play as it does in the real world. Symbolic play, however, uses objects to stand for other things – different from their primary use – for example, a bucket can be used as a hat. One thing may be substituted for another – conkers or shells for money. In symbolic play, imagined powers and properties are attributed to an object or person – a doll may 'speak'. Children may also refer to things that are not there, they may drive imaginary cars, or eat invisible food. Language requires both *concepts* and *symbols*. Make-believe relies heavily on verbalization, and symbolic players need to be more verbal to describe their play symbolism to others.

Children use 'physical' simile and metaphor in their play. An upturned scrubbing brush makes a perfect little hedgehog, its bristles impeccable prickles. Its likeness to the object suggests its use. Props become symbols too: a crown an instant metonym for a king or queen; an old rocking chair, with no seat, a boat; upturned baskets for bongo drums and later a barbecue; pegs for chips. As if reaching for a word or phrase to describe their experience, children pull together objects from the physical world to tell their stories. Their power of invention in the living language of their play can be truly staggering.

The ability to endow an object with a different order of existence is a genuine childhood talent. The child becomes the creator of the play object and invests something of herself in her creation: she has sought and found something there – a reflection of her own creative gift, perhaps. Pablo Picasso, in a process which mirrored this childhood activity, brought us the playful art of the 'found object' and opened our eyes to new ways of seeing – something we could learn equally well from our children, if only we would look.

The Playfulness of Children's Language

Sometimes there is a remarkable synergy between physical play – with its unorthodox use of materials – and the playful way children use language, which for them is still in a state of lively plasticity. A four-year-old boy, Charles, asked me to come outside to see his 'bout'. Puzzled, I said to him: 'What do you mean Charles, what is a "bout"?' He replied, 'It's a "bout" '. 'Do you mean a belt to put around your waist?', I asked. 'No, I mean a "bout" ', he persisted. At this point Charles decided I just wasn't getting it, so he took me to the sand-pit where a straight line and a circle had been carefully shaped out of the sand. 'Look Sally', he said, with polite exasperation: 'It's a *round-* a bout'.

> 'Once I saw it, it all made sense. Relief and triumph were written all over Charles' lovely face. I have made her

understand – at last! It was as if a "bout" was a place where things met and changed direction – a place where there might indeed be other kinds of bouts, square "a-bouts", or oblong "a-bouts", for example. (We do have the expression "about turn" and "thereabouts", so perhaps he was on to something.) He had a basic concept that the "about", as a noun, somehow stayed still whilst things happened in different ways around it, and was intuitively following the rules of grammar which apply when adjectives describe nouns. Charles was searching for a way to name the space.'[102]

The Playground of the Mind

Poetry, says Huizinga, 'proceeds within the playground of the mind'; it never loses its playful origins, its way of seeing:

> 'Poetry [is] bound by other ties than those of logic and causality... to understand poetry we must be capable of donning the child's soul like a magic cloak and of forsaking man's wisdom for the child's.'[103]

Children play with language. They reverse words, they rhyme, they play with alliterative and onomatopoeic sounds, and they create the most wonderful nonsense verse; they do this as naturally as they play with the shells and conkers around them. Image-making and personification belong to the mythopoeic frame of mind, says Huizinga – a non-literal way of seeing that is present in all ancient myths. Poetic language plays with images – it plays with a secret language. Huizinga cites the following examples from the Old Norse: 'speech-thorn' for tongue, 'floor of the hall of winds' for earth, 'tree-wolf' for wind.[104] One might think of 'boat-bearer' for the sea or 'journey carriers' for shoes, language-crafter for poet – immediately one's perception of the world begins to change. Some children's contributions, in the same vein, are: 'car-wheel-housie' for caravan, 'puff puff in the sky' for aeroplane, 'angel uniform' for a wedding dress.

A poetic way of seeing can be a salve to the rational mind. The old pre-scientific, poetic view speaks more to the feelings and the scientific view more to the thinking. As we have seen, when Ted Hughes describes the moon, he is deep in mythopoeic consciousness. He sees the full moon: 'looking' at his little daughter, Frieda, who points back at it herself. (See page 50)

"Moon!" you cry suddenly, "Moon! Moon!"
The moon has stepped back like an artist gazing
amazed at a work
That points at him amazed.

In the playground of his mind, Hughes personifies the moon as an artist. The breathtaking encounter between moon and child comes not from his scientific brain but from his poetic self. We need both ways of seeing the world and it is within the gift of language to help us achieve that, as the following story illustrates.

A child in my kindergarten came in with a large bump on his head. I asked him what had happened, and after a deep breath he began a fantastic tale about rescuing horses from a terrible fire (shades of 'Black Beauty' here); a tale which told of his bravery and courage in single-handedly saving a horse from certain death. The result of his valiant deed, he said, was the fearful (but heroic) injury which we now saw before us. This tale took a long time to tell and everyone listened with amazement. No one spoke, and when he eventually finished, an awe-struck silence filled the room. After a long pause he said, in a very different and rather small voice: 'Actually, I bumped my head on the bedroom door-handle.'

Children live in a state of consciousness where myth and reality interweave. My story-teller grew beyond himself in the telling of his tale and had us all spellbound in the process. He found no problem with the co-existence of his differing accounts. His embellishments made a fine story, which we all enjoyed, and in the telling of his tale, he had the opportunity to hone his story-telling skills. Returning to reality, we were given the bare bones of what had actually happened. Perhaps the bravery of the imagined story hero helped the child to deal with his real pain. No one questioned the inconsistencies between his two tales; indeed his young listeners seemed to accept that somehow, in different realms, both stories were true.

Learning to write letters at the age of four is one thing; having the imagination and verbal skill to create a story with character and plot, which comes to life for the listener, is something else altogether. Children deserve space and time to tell their tales; they deserve to enjoy and enrich their newly gained oral skills before being rushed on into something else. The playful pre-literate phase of childhood, where fluency in spoken language flashes with genius, is definitely a stage worth lingering over.

A child aged three invented a wonderful game: 'What would they say/do if…?' For example, 'What would a rabbit say/do if there was no water in the canal?' This game was quite challenging to her parents, who needed to make quick imaginative shifts to answer with the consciousness of, say, a rabbit or indeed any other creature. Caricatures or sentimental answers were not what the child wanted. What she wanted was a different way of seeing – a poetic image. Often the little girl supplied her own answers.

In the to-ing and fro-ing of their conversations, children also begin to play with logic. The 'if then' sentence below is an example.

Conversation between Joshua and Evelien

Joshua: 'Ghosts are people who have just died.'

Evelien: 'My grandfather's just died.'

Joshua: 'Then he must be a ghost.' [pause] 'Ghosts are bad.'

Evelien: 'My grandfather wasn't bad.'

Joshua: 'Then he won't be a ghost then, if you're bad you're a ghost.'105

Nina's Puppet Story

Nina (4-5): 'And he hanged it in his bedroom, where he hided it... "I shall get a bramble and stick it in your face", said he...' After a long time of patient waiting and really concentrated listening, Evelien whispers: 'When will it be my turn?'.

'When the snow has come... and gone away again', answers Nina dreamily. The story continues... 'But what did he see? Bright snowflakes falling on the ground.'

'Make a noise of snowflakes', says Evelien helpfully, drumming her own fingers on the table to make rather a heavy snowflake sound. 'The sun shined and shined on to the ground and the cloud came slappering down', says Nina.... Evelien watches and waits...

In this short extract from a very lengthy puppet story, which Nina and Evelien (who eventually got her turn) were telling to a rapt group of friends, Nina uses narrative and reported speech; she demonstrates an understanding of the past by using her own early forms of the past tense, 'hided' and 'shined'; and includes a brilliantly imaginative made-up word, 'slappering'. She uses repetition rather than adverbs for emphasis, as in 'the sun shined and shined'.

Nina's tale benefited from the presence of listeners: her *audi*ence – those who hear. The mouth needs the ear to help it speak, and it was the attentive ears of her friends, which helped Nina and Evelien's story to evolve. 'Listening' is a language skill; it is also an essential social skill. How much harder it is – to talk to someone who is not listening; it affects our ability to articulate and our self-esteem suffers. The importance of adults listening to children, and of children listening to them and to each other, is often underestimated. Serious play demands good listening skills.

In parody, 'that most refined form of jeering', children can rebel within safe parameters and savour the gymnastics of language. The reversed imagery in a carol I once heard parodied is funny and did not seem to detract from the correct version used in its more serious context. The words of the original song about Mary and Joseph on their way to Bethlehem are:

> "'I", said the donkey all shaggy and brown,
> "I carried his mother to Bethlehem town"';

and the parodied version:

> "'I", said the man all shaggy and brown,
> "I carried the donkey to Bethlehem town.'"

The ability to parody denotes a developmental stage, just as fluency in nursery rhyming does earlier. My kindergarten assistant, tall, thin and stately, whose first and second names were Jean and Elizabeth, was given the epithet 'Jean Bean Elizabeth the Queen' by a six year old. Not only had his jingle captured her qualities – beanpole-thin and regal – but it was also an excellent little rhyme in its own right. Not yet tied to the treadmill of letter learning this boy was free to enjoy his new-found ability with words.

David Elkind advocates 'horizontal enrichment' over 'vertical acceleration'. Accelerated learning, he contends, introduces totally new and abstract concepts which are alien and divorced from the child's current knowledge. Horizontal enrichment, however, spreads, elaborates, and deepens; children can consolidate and linger over their learning experiences.[106] This acceleration is exemplified in early literacy programmes based on a vertical model: climb as fast as you can and don't look left or right.

Language is necessary as a functional tool: it also frames the way in which we see the world for better or for worse. Grappling with letters too soon prioritizes one way of knowing over others, and undermines children's considerable oral skills. It takes away the pleasure of playing with words and the exquisite delight of subverting a newly mastered skill. It takes a little fun out of life.

The Art of Play

Children make wonderfully aesthetic 'scenes' in play. In my kindergarten many small worlds were created on the floor with simple objects: cloths, logs of all shapes and sizes (almost unlimited uses), pine cones (marvellous trees, and with sheep's wool on top – terrific ice cream cornets!), small wooden houses, boats, animals, green muslin veils for land, blue for water. We used few synthetic materials; wood is repairable, solid, and good to feel.

Both imitation and art require an eye for detail, a way of noticing salient features or characteristics of a subject. Children's play portrayals can sometimes reveal a delightfully idiosyncratic and humorous eye.

I watched a girl tell her friends she was going to be 'Rainbow the dog'. She adopted the standard hands-and-knees posture, the definitive first step in dog play, but what she did then was fascinating. She put out her tongue as far as she could, and then quite deliberately curled the bottom edge upwards. Complete with panting breath, the creature before us wagged itself into doggy life. The detail, the curling tongue, made all the difference.

The eye for detail is the artist's eye. It is the job of the teacher, or parent, to notice, as appreciative and silent critic (in the best sense of the word), the artist's eye in her children. Notice and be impressed, but inwardly, as unwanted praise can sometimes devastate unselfconscious re-creations.

When you are a child, you lack skill in technical draughtsmanship or the literary ability of an artist or writer. One of your amazing skills – easily underestimated by adults, and which requires neither canvas nor paper – is the ability to remake *yourself* in the image of that observed. I remember an incident in my own kindergarten which shows that even in childhood, the distinction between art and play is not easily made. Who can say where art begins and play ends?

A small boy had been to see a dolphin over the weekend; an experience which had strongly moved him. On Monday morning, he came to the kindergarten like a poet suffering under his muse, with a burning desire to express and re-create his thoughts and feelings and to relive his experience. With a sure touch, he took a long blue veil, spread it on the floor, lay upon it on his tummy, crossed his feet to make a tail and gently waved his legs up and down. His participation was so absolute and his imitation so perfect that you could almost hear the water lapping about his feet.

I felt as though I was witnessing the creation of a bodily poem or a beautiful piece of performance art. It was one small boy's personal homage to the dolphin which had so impressed him. In the 'art' of his play, his body and veil became his paint, palette, and canvas as, in his own 'childish' way, he brought his deeply felt experience to exquisite expression. His art was related to the meaning and truth of his experience and to his own existence.

Children engrossed in play are learning constantly. The parameters of their learning experience are unbelievably wide. The positive outcomes of play and the effects of the absence of the play experience are proven. Playing time is deeply significant for children's futures – yet play is under threat. The next two chapters look at childhood and at the ways in which it is being exploited: in the field of education, out of a misguided understanding of what the early years might be for in terms of the development of the whole, well-adjusted human being, and in the marketplace by large companies who target and manipulate children in a variety of ways for profit.

6. Whence the Playful Spirit of Childhood?

> 'To everything there is a season, and a time to every purpose under heaven.'
>
> Ecclesiastes

A colleague found the following old Suffolk recipe for 'Preserving Children'. Though somewhat bucolic and romantic, it speaks of a degree of freedom and a benign and playful adult attitude toward childhood seldom experienced in our times. Today's children are so rarely permitted their liberty. With smaller families and the cult of early adulthood, the custom of sending smaller children off for the day in the somewhat haphazard care of their older siblings no longer survives.

Recipe for Preserving Children

Ingredients:

    1 grass field

    1 dozen children

    Half a dozen dogs (and puppies if available)

    1 brook

    1 hundredweight (50 kg) of pebbles

Method:

Into the field pour children and dogs. Allow to mix well. Pour brook over pebbles, until slightly frothy. When the children are nicely brown, cool off in pebble froth. Dry. Serve with hot milk and freshly baked gingerbread.

Mrs Baron Clarke

In depressing contrast, today's recipe for childhood is all about containment:

'The daycare home is calm and pleasant. No major scenes, few conflicts. But boring. Everywhere one hears that play is vitally important, especially free play (…) but what do I see? I see children wandering around, playing a little bit of this, a little bit of that. They seem to be in a state of eternal waiting (…). The older children often do nothing. They hang around, maybe do some jumping, wait. They know there is no point in starting a game for they are sure to be interrupted.'

B. Olafson[107]

Real play is deep, absorbing, and satisfying. An active childhood, with plenty of opportunity for play, develops the individual child in innumerable ways, and is a wonderfully rich resource for the rest of life. Just as sunlight provides the body with vital nourishment, high-quality play in childhood is nature's vitamin for our whole sense of well-being. Our polarized society – in which we either work or are being entertained – has lost its playfulness. Wittingly or unwittingly, we impose our own standards on our children. We should not be complacent about the loss of play.

Steadily eating away at the play agenda, like moths in gauze, is the relentless pressure for children to be 'educated' at ever earlier ages. David Elkind argues that formal school programmes, which instruct very young children in subjects such as arithmetic and reading before they are ready, do not advance the child. In fact, they constitute a *mis*education. He cites the pediatrician and author, T. Berry Brazelton, who writes:

'The human infant is amazingly capable of compliance. He can be shaped to walk at nine months, recite numbers at two, read by three, and he can even learn to cope with the pressures that lie behind these expectations. But children in our culture need someone who will cry out, "At what price?"'[108]

The cost of accelerating childhood, of 'too much too soon', may be precocious and precarious entry into adulthood – and eventual overload. We may come to realize that the play-deficient child is a disadvantaged child. Can we reclaim childhood for our children? Libby Purves writes:

'… given sand, water, and a bucket an infant will unaidedly do physics, maths, resistant materials technology, design, hydraulics and (if burbling) language. A child burying an offending teddy head-first in the sand is doing ethics and drama; up-ending a bucket of water on his head is a fine training in comedy which may lead to a Bafta.

What is served by interfering with this personal curriculum because it is time to chant ABC or colour in tedious work-sheets? Adult convenience is served, certainly: and parental neurosis about education, and government statistics fed by measurable results. But you've wrecked the game and impoverished the child.'[109]

I am reminded of T. S. Eliot's question for our time:

Where is the life we have lost in living?

> *Where is the wisdom we have lost in knowledge?*
> *Where is the knowledge we have lost in information?*
>
> T.S. Eliot[110]

Early academics bring about what Elkind[111] calls a depletion of 'clock energy' – the energy we need for daily living. 'The early symptoms of stress associated with "clock energy" are fatigue, loss of appetite and decreased efficiency.' If early learning puts too much strain on children, they begin to dip into their reserves of 'calendar energy' (energy that is of a fixed quality for physical growth and maintenance of the body). Rudolf Steiner arrived at the same conclusion over seven decades ago, recognizing that forcing early intellectual powers in the child had a negative effect on organic processes within the body. In effect, *children become old before their time.*

The 'school child' must bend his or her will in a certain 'desirable' direction, a practice endorsed by that most autocratic of teachers, Gradgrind, in Dickens's novel *Hard Times*. Educators from Reggio Emilia in Italy have put together a chart that poses pairs of oppositions between the non-schooled child and the 'pupil'.

CHILDREN'S CULTURE	SCHOOL CULTURE
Ecological integration	Pedagogical isolation
Life development	Subject progression
Existential	Formal
Authentic	Second-hand
Time continuity	Time fragmentation
Canto ergo sum	*Cogito ergo sum*
Play	Study
Homo ludens	*Homo scribens*
Verbal	Books

To be in	To read about
Physical nearness	Physical distance
Try out own borders	Respecting others' borders
Self-understanding	Teacher evaluation
'I can already'	Feeling of not being able
Spontaneous	Planning
Extasis	Literal
Carpe Diem	Just wait – wait until you are big enough
Daring	Careful
Why, why, why?	What?
Empathic	Neutral
Creative	Sensible
1+1 rabbit = lots and lots of rabbits	1+1=2
Little blue horse	Big brown horse
Childlike	Rational
Improvisation	Prepared
Unexpected (the)	Expected
Original	Conform(ing)
Humour	[Seriousness]
Noise/sound-making	Silence
Senses	Intellectual
Physical movement	Physical stillness
I move, I learn	I sit, quietly
Egalitarian	Hierarchical
Free will	Forced upon
Without compromise	Negotiating
Dionysian	Apollonian
Musical	Logical
Courage	Insecurity
Engaged	Distant

Jon Roar, Reggio Emilia Educator[112]

Food for Thought: Children's Well-being

In her book on children's play, Heidi Britz-Crecelius writes:

> 'It is much less troublesome and exciting to teach the poor things to read already at kindergarten age. One does not need to get out of the armchair. The experts who lead the battle to teach children to read as early as possible emphasise again and again how much more quiet and well-poised early readers are than those who play – just as if quietness and poise were desirable in children! Well of course, the early readers can then read about all the things of which they have been deprived. But instead of assimilating experiences, they have information in their heads, and information is bound to be a quite inadequate substitute for experience.'[113]

The UK Mental Health Foundation's report *The Big Picture*[114] affords us an overview of the issues surrounding the emotional development and mental health of children and young people, uncovered during the last three years in the UK, examining over a thousand pieces of evidence. The study concludes that children are 'failing to thrive emotionally, are becoming less resilient and less able to cope with the ups and downs of life'. One in five children and young people aged four to twenty is estimated to suffer from mental stress, with problems ranging from bed-wetting to anorexia, significantly disrupting their lives. Pressures on children to succeed, and over-protection by parents who prevent healthy risk-taking, are factors in producing emotionally illiterate children who are at risk of breakdown. The curtailment of children's playtime and the strong emphasis on early learning leave children with very little time to develop emotional well-being.

In addition the report states that:

'there is evidence that the traditional rites of passage that used to apply for young people have significantly changed;

stresses on the family make it increasingly difficult for vulnerable parents to meet all their children's needs;

although children are on the whole physically healthier and better educated, they are more likely to experience unemployment, take drugs, experience parental separation or divorce, and to engage in criminal behaviour.'

The Big Picture concludes that:

'A truly child-nurturing society would be one where children were fully integrated rather than separated and where their needs were understood and were regarded as at least of equal importance as those of adults... We seem to have lost sight of what it feels like to be a child and of the connection between the child and the adult self.'

Television

Writing in the *Waldorf Research Journal* (IV, 1999) Dr Peter Struck expresses his concern about the physical effects of 'parking' children in front of the television:

'...children who have too seldom run and jumped, who have had insufficient opportunity to play on a swing or in the mud, to climb and to balance, will have difficulty walking backwards. They lag behind in arithmetic and appear to be clumsy and stiff. These children cannot accurately judge strength, speed, or distance; and thus they are more accident prone than other children.'

'[In Germany] …two thirds of all school children listen to music droning from gigantic boom boxes, Walkmen and Diskmen. Among elementary school age children, one in three already possesses his or her own television and one in five his or her own computer.'

'…one in ten adolescents already suffers hearing loss; 60% of children entering school have poor posture, 35% are over-weight, 40% have poor circulation. 38% cannot adequately co-ordinate their arms and legs, and more than 50% lack stamina for running, jumping and swimming.'[115]

Mud Pies Do You Good!

There are early indications that the increase in asthma and diabetes might be due to underexposure of the immune system to the microbacteria in the soil. If the immune system is not challenged by the world of germs, it begins to turn in on itself and attack the body's own organs. African children suffer relatively low levels of asthma, whereas in more affluent, hygienic countries asthma and diabetes are on the increase. Studies show that diabetes is less prevalent in children who have been exposed to more germs and have had more illness in their early years. Those who had been ill, particularly in the first year, were less likely to develop diabetes – a disease relating to a malfunctioning of the immune system. In our bodies, the majority of microbes we harbour are innocent; a good number are essential; and a relatively low number are bad for us. Grubby play, physical rough and tumble, and contact with others may be essential for the healthy functioning of the immune system.

Television keeps children inside, with the result that they are underexposed to the teeming world of helpful microbes: it also keeps them from the real world in other ways.

When adults watch TV, according Marie Winn, they refer to 'a vast backlog of real life experiences'. 'As the adult watches television', she argues, 'his own present and past relationships, experiences, dreams, and fantasies come into play, transforming the material he sees, whatever its origins or purpose, into something reflecting his own particular inner needs.'[116] Children, however, do not have this background of real-life experience and for many of them, television becomes the *primary* activity. Programmes are referenced by other programmes rather than by real experiences. *This is a devastating observation;* science fiction made fact. No alien abduction could be carried out with such efficiency and stealth. Whilst fragile identity is slowly sucked away, the absent self is re-constructed from the junk heap of piled-up perceptions pouring from the box, and a person whose memories, perceptions, and imaginations are essentially *borrowed* is created.

> 'It [the mind/self] is the difference between a room and my room — a space transformed by my belongings, associations and memories. To grow up, as Virginia Woolf might have said, is to acquire a mind of one's own.'
>
> Roy Porter[117]

Perhaps children also want and are surely entitled to a childhood of their own — a childhood less tainted by second-hand entertainment designed by adults. A cartoon expressing this sentiment depicts a young teenager, with his sad-looking mother in the background, in the process of smashing up the computer, in what appears to be a desperate attempt to find something. As the frustrated boy pulls the computer apart, he says: *'IT STOLE MY CHILDHOOD AND I WANT IT BACK.'*

The Culture of Childhood

The culture of childhood, as the prescient cartoon demonstrated, can be stolen. We are increasingly conscious of the need to protect and respect the range and diversity of cultures which together form the complement of human societies so that everyone's voice is heard. Yet how do you speak if you don't yet have a voice, if you can't yet articulate your thoughts, if you don't yet know what threatens you? If you are a child? Who speaks for the 'culture of childhood'? This fast-disappearing culture of childhood could once be found in all languages and in all human communities. The child's need to play remained the same the world over. Except in the formalized games, which we call 'sport', we adults find it very difficult to play: a different spirit moves us.

In his introduction to Gomme's book of childhood games, D. Webb recounts his experience of visiting a village in Portugal. It is a personal account which nonetheless strikes an all too familiar note:

'Twenty years ago I used to stay with a fisherman and his family in the Algarve of Southern Portugal. Every night from the neighbouring streets children came to the flat cobbled space in front of our cottage and sang and danced for an hour. I collected sufficient singing games to fill a book on its own. Today (April 1983) following the building of several luxury hotels and the tourist explosion, the fleet of fishing boats has vanished and the vast majority of cottages have been bought for holiday apartments. The narrow streets are clogged with parked cars. I visited an old lady who lived next door to our cottage, and one evening she collected a dozen or more children to come and do their singing games in the street. They did not know a single one. I asked a girl what they liked playing best, to which she replied: "Raiding the hotel for empty lipstick holders." '[118]

Webb wrote this in 1983 noting that: 'In less than two decades an entire tradition had been wiped out.'[119] He predicted a similar cultural shift in the UK, although not on such a catastrophic scale. Webb reckoned without the commercial explosion of the children's leisure industry and its subsequent hijacking of childhood.

Like others in this book, I was lucky enough to enjoy a carefree childhood. I played without fear through lanes, streets, parks and the odd bomb shelter, roaming around freely with my little tribe of friends from one location to the next. Whole days were spent with other children instead of adults – the choices and the rules of play were ours; they were self-imposed and carefully negotiated. Now, sadly, these important group experiences of childhood, with their own particular mores and codes of behaviour, have become subject to adult authority (albeit unwillingly). Sterile play areas replace their more haphazard but infinitely more interesting predecessors (when was the last time you saw a genuine child-built adult-free 'den'?), which offered a wealth of play experiences and encouraged the development of a wealth of differentiated faculties in the child. Nowadays, active adventures are replaced by simulated screen odysseys, with obvious implications for children's physical well-being; their social and imaginative development. As Neil Postman shrewdly observes,[120] watching television requires no skills, nor does it develop any.

Our adult world continues to make increasingly aggressive inroads into the playground of childhood as it flexes its muscles and assert its cultural dominance in a devastating variety of ways. There are precious few places where children can freely develop their own culture, and where the creative spirit of childhood can perform its magical transformations.

7. A Toy Story

> 'Unlike the obtrusive sports of men, for which ground has to be permanently set aside and perpetually tended, children's games are ones which the players adapt to their surroundings in the time available. In fact most street games are as happily played in the dark as in the light. To a child "sport is sweetest when there are no spectators". The places they like best are the secret places "where no one else goes"…To a child there is more joy in a rubbish tip than in a flowering rockery, in a fallen tree than in a piece of statuary, in a muddy track than in a gravel path… Yet the cult among his elders is to trim, to pave, to smooth out, to clean up, to prettify, to convert to economic advantage…'
>
> Opie and Opie[121]

The happiest people, claim Opie and Opie, are those who can rely on their own resources. When children begin to feel they can only enjoy themselves by playing with 'proper equipment', and if children's games are 'tamed and made part of school curricula', children will be dissatisfied and will descend into vandalism or the 'easy excitement' of rioting.

In July 2000, 10,000 children turned up on the second day of the imaginatively designed Diana, Princess of Wales, Playground in Kensington Gardens. The original playground was funded by children's author J. M. Barrie, at the beginning of the last century. The new playground boasts a pirate ship, some wigwams, and paddling areas – but no high technology and there are no product lines for sale. The queues were over an hour long. It was do-it-yourself fun and it was free. Some children came complete with capes and swords, ready to play on the replica wooden 'Jolly Roger' ship. Tim Davies, aged 8, said, 'I wish all parks were like this'.[122] Notwithstanding the publicity and uniqueness of this particular playground, it would seem that the phenomenal response from the children expresses some kind of need. A need for places, all kinds of places, where children can make believe.

In the past, many children tended to made their own toys, the creative spirit of play simply using whatever was to hand, as the following examples illustrate. The first, from a book entitled *A Century of Childhood,* is from Mary Brown, the daughter of a textile worker in Halifax, born during the First World War.

> 'The games we played needed no money spent on them. For a skipping rope I used to get a rough straw rope from the boxes of oranges given away by greengrocers. These boxes had two compartments and we used them for bookcases or dolls' houses. We made dolls' furniture from matchboxes and cotton reels. We lived near the roadside and I used to copy the boys and put pins on the tramlines. When they were flattened we pushed them through bits of matchsticks and said they were swords.'[123]

The second example is from Sylvia Land, born in war-ravaged Sheffield after the Second World War:

> 'I vividly remember playing 'chip shop' with broken slates for fishcakes, broken bricks for fish and sand and rubble for

chips. Play shops were made out of mountains of bricks and empty cans were threaded with precious string and formed into a loop to make mini-stilts.' 124

Intelligence, invention, resourcefulness, and imagination were the lifeblood of these games. It would be foolish to suggest that life was easy for many of these children: it wasn't, but they had something which children of today lack – their games still formed part of a culture independent of the adult world... the culture of childhood.

In his book *The Development of Play*, David Cohen presents many different perspectives on toys. He quotes the French semiologist Roland Barthes, who sees toys as 'the stunted hallmarks of a materialistic culture'. He claims that commercial toys make the child passive, a user rather than a creator; and that the toys we produce for our children reveal the list of things the adult world does not find unusual – war, bureaucracy, ugliness, Martians. His psychological point is that children should devise *their own* games, and not have them prepared for them. He deplores the attempts by the commercial market to turn children into passive consumers.125

Ready-made toys may be perfect miniature replicas of the real thing (although they are far more likely to be caricatures), but they stunt the imagination and may dull the child's individual transformative powers by narrowing perspectives of seeing. Many children have toy compulsions: 'Thomas the tank engine' dominated the waking life of one child I taught. He woke in his Thomas bed, slept between Thomas sheets, drew Thomas curtains, ate from Thomas plates, and lived in a Thomas world. His parents felt that he was playing imaginatively, but it seemed to me that his capacity to envision was overloaded with one type of image, and that his play had become stereotyped. He was only able to play what he had seen, and although he loved his trains and played quite creatively within this framework, the parameters of his imagination had become proscribed by the Thomas experience.

The phenomenal success of Barbie, produced in large enough numbers to circle the world at least seven times, is symptomatic of our times. Already sexualized, she requires little of the mothering or fathering element which dolls and soft toys traditionally elicited from their owners. Barbie is the ultimate consumer doll. In a brilliant marketing strategy, 'must have' items of fashion and lifestyle accessories for each doll are marketed to Barbie owners, potentially locking little girls into serial purchasing or feelings of inadequacy. The Barbie experience establishes shopping 'needs' and buying patterns in childhood. These patterns may continue into adulthood, in a seamless process, which prioritizes *having* over *being* – an attitude to life, which Erich Fromm explores in his remarkable book *To Have or to Be*. Barbie, with her stunning looks and impossible figure may also tie little girls prematurely into the idea of 'image'. 'Image consciousness' is a major marketing tool for clothing, make-up, and lifestyle companies, and a source of anguish and insecurity for a great number of adolescent girls.

'Pester power', in which companies target children as a means of pressurizing adults, produces real financial reward. It is no secret that advertising agencies are ruthlessly engaged in a full-scale assault upon childhood. Loaded with weapons of deception – with gimmickry and illusion – they target children's vulnerabilities and those of their parents, to serve their own ends. The delightfully idiosyncratic and unpredictable fads of childhood are now deliberately stage-managed for profit.

The strategic campaign to advertise and sell Pokémon cards is a case in point. After high TV profiling, certain cards were deliberately limited to increase desirability and rarity value. This led to bullying and acts of desperation amongst children. A seven year old offered to swap his first newly pulled baby tooth, presumably because of its under-the-pillow value; his gap-less friends refused it, sensing credibility problems at home perhaps. But what else had he to offer? Another boy went so far as to offer his sister in exchange for the desired card.… Why do we reduce children to this desperate and humiliating state? Enhanced or reduced status and self-esteem become synonymous with the possession, or lack of, the right products. Manipulative advertisers understand this painful social dynamic and employ it in an abuse of power. Our children, who rightly own nothing and thus everything, are being cynically reduced and degraded by their own exploited feelings.

Toys are important to children who invest them with life forces. The picture of the lively kicking baby, whose limp and lifeless doll lies in the cot beside him, changes as he grows. As he masters and controls his own limbs, he uses his imaginative and cognitive abilities to animate his doll. At about 24 months the child becomes still, and the doll 'plays'. This is a wonderful transference, the child imaginatively bestowing beingness upon the doll. This is a uniquely human attribute, a huge imaginative leap. Plato and others have described play in animals as a 'leap' – a free movement. In human play this kind of doll animation requires a 'leap' of the imagination.

Piaget recognized the importance of the doll. Referring to his own daughter, he wrote: 'We can be sure that all happenings, pleasant or unpleasant, in the child's life will have repercussions on her dolls.'[126] Children can, through the medium of the doll, rehearse events, recapture their fears and worries, take risks, and indulge in those behaviours normally prohibited.

Dolls are significant in other ways, as the following story illustrates.

Recently, I was fortunate enough to meet a fascinating woman – the angel collector in Chapter 4 – whose memories of a 1950s childhood are still exceptionally clear. Not only was she able to remember the details of what she had actually done, she was also able to recapture the thoughts and feelings she had experienced as a child.

Her mother worked full time and the girl and her beloved boy cousin spent a great deal of their free time exploring their local area together. Setting off on foot for the day, with a Camp Coffee bottle full of lemonade powder and water and some boiled egg sandwiches, the two friends went wherever their fancies took them. Sometimes they played in the real world and sometimes in the world of their own imaginations, often in both. I asked her how it had felt to have the freedom go off and play like this. 'We were kings and queens', she said; 'the world belonged to us.' What struck me once more, as it had whilst listening to Jack's tale (see 'Beginnings', page 1) was how independent and empowered these children had been; during the hours they spent together, they were indeed rulers of their realm.

The two were great explorers and loved to negotiate the local waters together. The girl would inveigle the boy into tackling the overgrown, bramble-strewn 'rapids' to secure a trifling something for her – a special insect or a stickleback, perhaps. Invariably, as he waded into the (shallow-ish) depths, the water would rise above the level of his wellies, soak his socks, and waterlog his feet. For this, he received a cuffing back at home.

She also remembered a shed at the bottom of her garden where she and some other girls had played dolls. For this game, she said: 'We didn't seem to need husbands, or boys to play them, it was just the girls together.'

Did her dolls have different characters, I asked? 'Of course they did!', she replied – the long forgotten pride of a nine-year-old mother flashing once again across her face. 'They were my family!' It struck me that she had conceived and brought her little family to birth in her imagination, just as later she would conceive and bear her own children. She had given her dolls life.

She went on to describe the personalities of her first children for me. So vivid was her account and so real her descriptions that I felt were I only to look I would see them there still, sitting patiently in the garden shed, waiting for their small mother's return.

Dinah, a pot doll with 'red-painted rosebud lips and painted-on hair', was a 'baby, a heavenly baby'. Her face was 'really good'. She was precious because of her fragility and because she was given to the child by her grandmother. 'She was often in the poorly bracket.' She had a quiet personality, and 'because she was so fragile I never felt I got to know her properly'. At this point, we both realized that the qualities ascribed to Dinah also applied to a person we had spoken of earlier. This woman, like Dinah, needed careful handling. She too was fragile, difficult to get to know, and precious. It seemed that Dinah, the doll, had also functioned as a metaphor for a certain type of person. The doll's composition: cold and delicate china, her persona, fragile and impeccably presented, and her genesis, a special gift from Gran, had elicited a self-consciously careful response from the girl. Now, in adult life, she was able to draw upon these same skills in her careful 'handling' of a similarly fragile woman.

Elizabeth was the beauty of the family – she had dark hair, which was pulled back. Barbara was about 3 feet (one metre) tall and a more grown-up doll: she was naughty, she wouldn't go to sleep, and she was smacked. 'I used to feel quite cross with her.' Clutey was a rubbery doll – 'She was the Personality Doll, you could do anything with her'. On Friday nights, when the child was given her weekly dose of Syrup of Figs (to move the bowels), the dolls too were given their draught, which was administered with firmness, by their small mother, despite their protestations – just as Piaget notes. As a child born just after the war, she had been very concerned about her dolls' welfare – if the bombs were to return, would they feel frightened? Her worry on their behalf may have been a way of alleviating her own fears. Protective feelings can be a defence against fear and powerlessness in oneself; and it is possible to become a braver person on another's behalf.

Her childhood doll-play taught her nurturance; it also taught her to become a good judge of character. She learnt too that there are many other 'selves' in the world – all valid and all different. Through her own imagination and the assimilation of observable data, she was learning about the me and the not-me. 'I will always remember their characters. They were my family', she said wistfully, 'Oh I loved them. I wish I still had them now'.

Her friend, the boy cousin, had a Teddy whose head had come off. He didn't seem to mind it that way at all – in fact he rather liked it. Teddy would come bouncing down the stairs in two bits, and he would play happily with the body – with or without the head. He was a divergent non-materialistic thinker! He strongly opposed his mother's wish to throw it away. He loved his Teddy for reasons other than its outer form. This boy was remarkably inventive; he could see what was beyond the visible and imagine alternatives – he could solve problems. He was and is an individual thinker.

I wondered whether the magical thinking exhibited above would be possible with today's heavily branded, themed dolls. I suspect that the snappy, computerized, programmed toys of today offer

Doll Play

children a bleaker, more alienated future – as chillingly forecast in the following passage:

> '...talking to a teddy bear that responds in a distorted recorded voice seems less appealing to us than listening to a child talk to a bear and then supply the bear's response in his own "bear" voice. The ultimate travesty we envision would involve two bears (triggered by a child) talking to each other in a playroom, each one repeating one another's words....' [127]

Here the child *watches* a toy talk to a toy. He programmes and watches but does not necessarily interact or play. What need is there for him to do so? The toys already have characters. Digitally programmed talking teddies are probably at the benign end of the market, but if these kinds of toys are resistant to the child's imagination and love, the repercussions may be far-reaching.

On a positive note, the introduction of 'Persona dolls', with a range of 'skin' colours, or a missing limb, perhaps, or some other feature, representative of the many varieties of people who make up our communities, is to be welcomed. These dolls, each with their own stories, are used to help children play out situations they might be experiencing in their lives, or to prepare them for new ones. Playing with a doll who is different from you helps prepare you to meet a real child or adult with the same difference.

According to Richard Hyman, the chairman of Verdict, the leading retail consultancy group, 'There has been a fundamental shift in the psyches of children'. Children who, a couple of generations ago, felt lucky to get anything, now want 'things with currency'.[128]

These shifts are reflected by toy retailers. The world's biggest toy shop, Hamleys, established 260 years ago, is in trouble: its shares have dropped by 20 per cent and at the time of writing, it had issued four profit warnings in the previous 24 months. This is because, as Hyman puts it:

'Something that would once have been a great present for a seven year old just won't do any more.... Kids are turning their backs on toys, or at least toys as we once knew them. They are fickle. They are opinionated. They want lifestyle accessories – a Manchester United shirt or something they can do on the internet. No group of consumers has ever changed its tastes as quickly and completely as modern children.'[129]

Why do they want these things, I wonder? One significant reason is that toy retailers engineer fads through the medium of television and the internet. It seems to me that children do not and are not able to make relationships with their toys today; their function has more to do with acquisition, status, and brand image:

'Frequently how well a toy sells has nothing to do with its intrinsic qualities and everything to do with its packaging and associations. Hot movies and slick marketing will move the goods, but not always and not necessarily for long. Toys used to be handed down through generations. Now they are junked before their batteries have run out.'[130]

Dr Jane Prince, Principal Lecturer in Psychology at the University of Glamorgan, argues that this is part of a disturbing trend which signals that most children no longer know how to play. Electronic gadgets prevent them from creating play-worlds. Assessment at school is constant, affecting the freedom and time to play, and children's spontaneity; parents feel the pressure to buy educational toys (which may promote only one side of a child's total development and actively neglect others).

The power of television determines the sort of toys that children want to own. Instead of inventing their own adventures or personalities for their toys, children re-enact what they have seen on television.

Toys often overwhelm children. Curtis describes a study by Ishigaki,[131] which compared the number of toys owned by Japanese and Israeli children. Israeli children boasted an average of 11 toys per head, whereas the Japanese felt they were deprived if they had around 45.

True creativity, however, has been linked to 'low structure materials': I have seen children playing with very simple materials which, because of their non-fixedness, inspired the children to use them in a number of highly imaginative and symbolic ways. My daughter once made a marvellous queen from a pair of folded white socks. The folded knot was a face, a rubber band the crown, and the dangly bits her robes – the puppet made me laugh and marvel. Human creativity is splendid when improvising.

In her book, *Child in the Forest,* Winifred Foley describes her childhood play during the 1900s in the 'ashmix', the village dump which, because there were no dustmen at that time, became the repository for all the village rubbish – and thus an irresistible attraction to children who are great natural recyclers. Using 'rubbish', they played creatively and symbolically, if not hygienically, for hours.

'The ashmix consisted mainly of buckets of ashes, with empty tins, broken china, and bottomless pails…. Older girls pillaged the ashmix for tins, bottles, and bits of china to play "houses" or "shops". Nearby stood a great chestnut tree, one alone among a forest of oak; each triangle among its roots was a girl's territory. A bit of rusty iron bed lath, balanced on a stone with a cocoa lid on each end made scales. We sold "brown sugar" (sandy earth), "boiled sweets" (little stones), and "currants" (sheep droppings).'

Winifred Foley[132]'

Dr Peter Blachford, a researcher at the University of London Institute of Education, who is currently looking at the range and diversity of children's games, was quoted in the *Times Educational Supplement* as saying: 'If the vocabulary of play is impoverished, the implications are serious indeed... we mess with playtime at our peril'.[133]

Part of this 'vocabulary' has been usurped, as outlined above, by the ever-expanding toy industry. Nowadays, 'less' is definitely not perceived as 'more.' It wasn't always so. Writing in 1916, Norman Douglas, another collector of children's games, observed: 'It all comes to this: if you want to see what children can do, you must stop giving them things. Because of course they only invent games when they have none ready made for them.'[134] Although this is a somewhat extreme view – after all, we give toys and games to our children because we love them, and there are any number of games for children on the market – Douglas does have a point. Indeed, recent research in Germany has given strong credence to Douglas's view:

'Der Spielzeugfreie Kindergarten research project [the German 'nursery without toys'], where children are, within reason, left to their own devices with spartan resources (blankets, tables, chairs etc.) at certain times during their nursery education, nurtures imagination, interactive skills, a sense of purpose, and an ability to concentrate on tasks... And because these activities reflect their own stages of development and ability – rather than an arbitrarily imposed norm – they are able to feel good about their own achievements, and the learning process itself.' [135]

New research also suggests that children are losing the ability to play properly because they are being given too many toys and games. Claire Lerner, a childhood development researcher with

Zero to Three, which is funded by the US government to run pre-school educational programmes across America, writes: 'Our studies show that giving children too many toys or toys of the wrong type can actually be doing them harm. They get overwhelmed and cannot concentrate on any one thing long enough to learn from it.' Kathy Sylva, Professor of Educational Psychology at the University of Oxford, supports this view: 'When they have a large number of toys there seems to be a distraction element and when children are distracted they do not learn or play well.'[136]

Small children, to the surprise of their parents, sometimes prefer the imaginative possibilities of the box their present came in, to the toy itself. The unsullied imagination delights in simplicity.

The sketch below was copied from a painting of Indonesian children, and shows a small boy enjoying the simple pleasures of a home-made banana leaf hobby horse A marvellous horse for a boy or girl – despite its transitory nature.

A mother told me how her child had once played a game of 'Postman' (not Postman Pat, just Postman child). The slatted back of a dining chair became his post box: he made his own letters and tiny stamps, complete with queen's head (of sorts); he borrowed a hat and cloak, made himself a silver foil badge, and played for hours at delivering letters to various destinations around his house. A kind aunt, having seen his obvious delight in the game whilst visiting, later bought him a manufactured toy 'Postman Set' from the shops nearby... but he never played with it. The charm of his own play lay in his creative participation and in his ability to transform; each little invention brought its own pleasure, and enabled the child to add something of himself to the game.

Mass production of toys

'From bicycles and building blocks to doll carriages and hoops and tops, the world of children in Victorian art is a world of commercial, mass produced, isolating toys. Whether in the solitude of the nursery or outside on the front lawn or in the park, the 19th century child – separated from the life of his elders – was literally surrounded by his toys – dozens of them – his loneliness assuaged only by the new materialism of childhood.'

A. Schorsch[137]

Elizabeth Stutz, founder of 'Play for Life', has campaigned tirelessly for the rights of children to be granted time and space to really play. In an article published in 1995, she writes:

'Saturation entertainment has taken over the playtime and the home life of children, so that, not only do they suffer the consequences of being overwhelmed and brutalised by their

entertainment, but they are exposed to concepts totally
unsuitable for and inimical to their stage of development, and
– in addition – they are robbed of the carefree hours in which
they should be enjoying the nourishing and creative forces of
play.... Children's leisure time has been made the subject of
intense commercial competition. The richest and most powerful

industries and interest groups, such as the ever expanding communications industry, the electronic entertainment and music industries ...the toy and consumer goods and food empires, these have together in a loose conglomerate taken over as their domain, the market of childhood and youth; they decide what children will play, read, eat, wear, admire, hate, how they behave to each other, to their parents and authority and who their role models are to be; this contrivance is then sold as the youth culture.' [138]

'Where is the child's voice in all of this? The commercially produced youth culture is at risk of creating a 'herd mentality' whereby everyone is compelled to eat the same grass, graze the same field, drink from the same trough. The culture of childhood, on the other hand, gradually brings about the birth of the unique individual.

[Rousseau suggested that]... we select [children's] educational diet by reference to what he called their "childish interests" rather than to the subjects we adults feel they ought to learn – whatever the reasons for our choices. We should not do what he says most educationalists do, who are "always looking for the man in the child, without considering what he is before he becomes a man"... we must respect what Charles Dickens once called "the childhood of the mind", and accept his warning against the possibilities of injuring this.

Rousseau knew that children have their own ways of seeing, feeling, and thinking, and that working with their 'inclinations' was the best way to promote their education. The child shouldn't be adapted to the curriculum, it should be the other way round. '[139]

One of the best ways of understanding children's play is by remembering how you played as a child. Even when people say they can't remember a thing, after thinking for a while, to their surprise, the play memories do usually come back. I have done this exercise with many people and it usually proves to be quite an emotive experience: a link with a self, long forgotten. It helps in empathizing with children today. The next chapter is a resumé of one of these workshops.

8. A Charter for Children's Play

'Play in childhood is an exceedingly complex phenomenon. It is an activity which combines into a single whole very different strands of thought and experience. Many of these persist in adult life.'

Margaret Lowenfeld[140]

This chapter results from an international workgroup on play held in Dornach, Switzerland in October 1999. Our ambitious aim was to discover why play might be important to us as human beings: why it matters and where it belongs in the human soul and spirit. More and more, as the pressure for early academic instruction intensifies, as television and video dominate the imagination, the participants felt we need to be able to speak about the importance, indeed the *genius* of play. What resulted was a 'tip of the iceberg experience', an opening of doors long since closed, and the beginnings of a new consciousness of the importance of our childhood play, both in childhood itself and subsequently. We wanted to make a charter for play that would respect the child and the 'childhood of the mind'.

We began by looking at the small-scale research in a Steiner kindergarten in England (see page 78), which showed children creating some 54 different themes of play over a period of 11 days. The children observed were passionate players, their play quixotic and exciting. It made us conscious of the pre-eminence of play in the early years and of the challenge: *Can I grasp their world, nourish their imaginations, give my children physical and soul space to play? Can I preserve a space for their freedom, for their spiritual selves to grow and develop? We thought about the mystery that imagination changes reality and imagination is also changed by reality.* We spoke about imagination, inspiration, and intuition and the way to 'the other' through 'empathy play' (see Chapter 3).

In our workshop, we used ourselves as 'ex-children' (it was Iona Opie who first described herself as an ex-child) as research material by recalling our own childhood play experiences. We were struck by the intensity of our memories and of the power those long-forgotten games still have in our minds and souls. We tried to feel the way they might have helped to weave the patterns of our individual destinies. Our intention as an international group – with participants from Canada, Finland, the USA, Denmark, Sweden, the UK, and Switzerland – was to produce a *Charter for Play* that would be relevant to all cultures and all nations. Each memory would produce a word or phrase for our charter.

The following are extracts from the stories told.

SAFE GROUND

I liked to play outside, knowing it was safe because my mother was nearby. If she wasn't there I couldn't play so well; she provided the safe ground for me. I didn't need to see her and she didn't intrude – just knowing she was there was enough. Often there was more fun in making the rules for games than in playing them. I learned to know my surroundings, the lie of the land, the shortcuts, and long winding ways. I learned to become social; to gain understanding of the other children – even of the fights between the boys.

RELATIONSHIP

I remember carrying out operations on my bear at the age of five or six – a time when I was in hospital myself. He was a big bear, which I cut and sewed up again, and his insides were made of sawdust. I loved cooking, and 'real' play – hairdressing with real scissors (and real cutting!). Relationships were so important to me, both between child and child and child and teacher. I liked to have a special friend. In the kindergarten I was told to sleep whether I wanted to or not. If I couldn't sleep I was smacked. I liked to play at being a ballerina.

DISCOVERY

I liked to be able to play in the forest alone – to be able to play alone. I liked playing with my brother, with the elements, with mud. I loved the outdoor life in all its seasons. Nature was a mystery world where you could be alone without fear. I loved the colours, the leaves, the dirt, the mud, the sense of dryness and of wet. I always wanted to know, 'What's around the next rock?'.

IMAGINATION

I played with my sister – dolls in bed – and with many other children at kings and queens. I loved tiny berries and big rocks. Each rock was a piece of a kingdom, a huge rock a castle. In my imagination there was a beautiful lady whom I always expected to come alive. She almost did, she became so real. My imagination was so exciting.

PRIVACY

I lived in a country village where my parents worked in a little grocery store. My little brother and I liked to do everything my parents did. We played shops and with the village children. We spent our summers near a lake, where I experienced the freedom to develop a strong relationship to Nature. I liked having my own spaces; places for privacy.

NEW ME

I lived in the countryside in a house with a garden and was depressed when we moved to the city. I played with dolls, walked, dressed-up in my mother's clothes, and danced, mostly by myself. I felt in my play that I could meet a new me – another self.

MAKING

I lived in the countryside near a baker's, in a little village. I liked to make little cakes – with mud and leaves – and we built an elaborate oven. I was interested in the idea of making things to sell. Nature and outside were very important to me.

FEARLESSNESS

I grew up in the suburbs of Texas and I had three little brothers. We played with a neighbouring girl in the yard at the back. Life was a bit constrained and held, although we had imaginatively free adventures climbing up and down the pile of bricks in the yard. Our adventures involved going up and down (the bricks), exploring an unknown world. My imaginary life was very alive. Our inner freedom made us strong. We were fearless; we had bold adventures and called ourselves 'THE GREAT GIRLS'. We spent hours on 'mastery play', becoming experts at 'Jacks'.

TRANSFORMATION

I loved marbles, with their beautiful colours. I thought the squiggles, whirls, and swirls inside them were magical. We developed skills and kept trophy marbles in a big jar. I was the eldest child of four, with two sisters and a brother. We would transform ourselves into princes and princesses, rolling out the rug to make a procession. I remember this ability to transform and I remember colour – light and colour.

From these rich gleanings we created a **Charter for Children's Play.**

Charter for Children's Play

Children play best:

When adults are watchful but not intrusive, when safe ground lends courage to their discoveries and adventures.

When their trust in life is whole, when they welcome the unknown, and are fearless.

When the world is shared with them. When there are places and spaces they can make their own.

When their games are free from adult agendas and when their transformations require no end-product.

When their senses are directly engaged with Nature and the elements.

When they are free to become gatherers, makers, and world creators in their own time and in their own ways.

When they can play with others and make relationships.

When they can play alone, be solitary and private.

When they can become new selves through their play with others and in their own imaginings.

When they can reveal themselves, their joys, sufferings, and concerns, without fear of ridicule, and when mystery and imagination are not denied by fact.

Our charter helped us to realize the value of our own play, and to highlight its central place in all of our childhood. Some people began to make links between their childhood play and their later adult choices.

We began to see that play should indeed be recognized as the central activity of childhood, particularly if it leads to freedom and to the ability to fulfil destiny intentions. A child who is not free to play will struggle with independence later in life. Educators who think equipping children with academic skills earlier and earlier will make them independent may be misguided. As Ralph Waldo Emerson[141] said, *Intuition* [through play] should come before *tuition*.

We looked at how differently each child plays in the context of Rudolf Steiner's comments on play:

> 'We should not introduce standardization into the upbringing of children, especially not in play. We must allow play to be individualistic. We must give special attention to what the talents and interests of each child are, for otherwise we would sin... Spirit and soul must be independent in play so that material things have no effect.'[142]

and

> 'Through play, children have a free but definable manner of acting upon the human soul constitution. Play and the accompanying soul activity of the young child arise from a deep consciousness of what truly constitutes the nature and essence of the human being.'[143]

We looked briefly at the work of Tina Bruce, an Early Years university professor and passionate advocate for play, in England, who recommends tracking the play of individual children; looking at the self-chosen 'schemas' they are involved in – for example, enveloping, enclosing, trajectory play, etc. She believes particular themes and forms recur, and that the child works for a time with a kind of muse, then moves on to something else. The same forms and patterns, she suggests, resurface, for example, on the floor with pieces of wood, in bread-making, in movements, and in drawings. For a further explanation of schemas please see Cathy Nutbrown's *Threads of Thinking.*[144]

We spoke of Piaget's recognition of the importance of play, and of his attention to imitation as a force for learning and for the development of feelings. We thought about the importance of the child as creator, of the lifeless doll by the baby's side, which later becomes the animated doll given life by the toddler.

We then tried to establish what conditions would best serve healthy free play. What makes play possible? Our suggestions are set out below:

It was felt that boys found creative play difficult and that they need materials to build; it was felt that boys should have opportunities to build every day.

There is a need for flexibility of materials – for example, a rocking chair without a seat made a wonderful boat which provided hours of play for a group of boys.

Boys don't usually build houses. In our experience, they build ships, cars, rockets (which look just like houses!) but which are called by different names!

Children should play without fear of ridicule.

Risk is healthy – some controlled risk is good.

Children need opportunities to play in a threefold way to develop different spheres:

–   Cultural/civil – puppets, drama performances;
–   Political/rights – territory/tribal, war games (with caveats);
–   Economic – shops, barter.

Much children's play can be seen as a re-creation of the journey through humankind's history.

Working adults are a great incentive to children's play. They should draw back from direct involvement where possible.

Adults need to be brave and tolerant whilst ensuring safety.

They need to be careful not to intervene in disputes too soon – children are often able to transform situations themselves.

Children need to have opportunities to self-challenge in their play.

Toys were not felt to be of as much value as 'things'. The value was in the activity, not in the beautiful or perfect toy. Often the things we have discarded supply the imagination with the greatest incentive to play.

Children need time to play; sometimes even those who value play hurry them out of their play.

They need plenty of outside play – in all seasons.

Little children need their space and time to play. We have noticed that the youngest children often begin to play when the older ones begin to clear up.

Children who can't play need their life sense activated. Distress and illness prevent children from playing.

Children are often afraid to play for fear of failure.

Moveable story pictures help play – they are flexible and allow soul-breathing.

Adults need to develop the right kinds of ears to hear when play is healthy, and when otherwise. Children like to play out of sight.

We need to be conscious when play becomes obsessive and to learn what each child's play has to tell us about his/her developmental stage, and social and emotional well-being.

Children should be owners of their free imaginations and not bound by inflexible rationality: fear and sometimes exhaustion can come from too much explanation.

If necessary, play should be allowed to rest for a while during the 5 to 6 year old stage.

We then looked briefly at baby play, which deserves much greater attention, well beyond the scope of this book. However, we did conclude that for play to function, babies needed the following.

Warmth, food, sleep; bodily comfort.

People and peace; to be in the vicinity of others yet also to have genuine times of peace.

Committed individuals who give them time.

Babies play best, we all agreed, when they are comfortable, happy, and *loved*. If they feel they are truly met at feeding, nappy-changing and cuddling times, then play will arise spontaneously out of surplus happiness forces. Neglected children, in orphanages for example, cease to play. One of the signs of returning to health in a sick child is that he or she will begin to play. All play ceases when the sense of life is depressed.

The next chapter looks at our adult attitude to play and what we can do to help. I offer it as a beginning, not a solution.

9. Children Need People Who Will Sanction Play

Children Are Different Today

'Britain's youngsters rule the roost in the home with more power and influence than any previous generation' is the lead line introducing a survey commissioned by the Abbey National Bank (UK) of 950 families.[145] The survey found that the family was becoming more democratic. Relationships were more open, children were involved in decision-making, and their views were treated with respect.

Children's views, it reports, are sought on a wide range of family issues including choice of evening meal – nine out of ten 'dictate' what that should be – new car, annual holiday, re-decorating, moving home. Much, but not all, of this is good news: children's voices do need to be heard. However, the not-so-subtle marketing agenda is clear. Choice has its price: 'We are amazed at how much influence children have on family life. Their views and opinions are treated with respect, *which has huge ramifications for companies.* Children will have greater power and influence than ever before' (my emphasis). It seems to me that 'children's choice' is not about their freedom to play or explore, inventing and creating their own democratic games and toys. It is about their buying power. The child is now the customer.[146]

Companies have unprecedented access to children's hearts, minds, and souls – a direct line to the living room where they can influence children's 'choices' by seductive marketing techniques. Five year olds think that advertisements are there 'to tell you things'; not until eight do they realize that an advert is a selling device. Does this actually leave children with more choice or with less choice? Are they more free or less free?

'The notion of individual ability presupposes that the child is capable of choice and of making decisions. With that assumption, the capitalist has no scruples about selling to children. "Let the buyer beware" should hold for the child as well as the adult. Yet capitalistic exploitation of children today is every bit as harmful and pernicious as it was in the time of the Industrial Revolution, when children's physical abilities were exploited and their physical health was put at risk. Today's children's psychological abilities are being exploited and their mental health is being put at risk.'

David Elkind [147]

Elkind's concerns are based on realities. The market for highly salted and sugared foods, such as crisps and popcorn, is aimed at children. The unhealthiness of the foods is secondary to the fact that they 'cater to children's tastes', thus encouraging children to make their parents buy them. The same is true for the sale of war toys to children, which 'reflects the same subordination of child welfare by making a profit'.

Playing for Time

'There must be a key person who [values] and sanctions children's play and accepts the child's inventions with respect and delight. There must be a place for play, a "sacred space" (no matter how small), and time.'

Singer and Singer[148]

Children across all socio-economic groups have become dispossessed of their play spaces. The fields and streets are quiet. The play space for many is the computer console or the area in front of the television.

As Singer and Singer point out, play spaces can be very small. My son once spoke about the end of the world at the bottom of his bed: his diminutive play space was no less sacred for that – in fact it encompassed the whole world. Play spaces are everywhere, waiting for children to find them. Giving children time to play takes a change in attitude, a re-alignment of priorities, and a willingness to respect and delight in things that to adult eyes might just look like a mess. *Look closer!* Investment in playtime will reap dividends.

Children's well-being is enhanced by their play: their bodies are exercised, their imaginations stimulated, their cognitive skills developed, and they can rest afterwards. In contrast, inactive children become listless but not tired. Television stimulates the nervous system but fails to tire the body in a healthy way. Consequently children don't sleep well, and a cycle of problematic behaviour is soon set in motion.

A teacher colleague of mine working in London was so concerned about her class's lack of ability to play that for their homework she told them to go home and build a den. They announced to their surprised parents, 'Mrs Ginn says we've got to make dens'. Mattresses were dragged from beds, chairs and tables upturned, sheets were draped everywhere, and a crop of dens sprung up like mushrooms. The children enjoyed themselves tremendously, and were far livelier in their work as a result. Order was soon restored at the various homes, although the children were keen to repeat their experience.

One den, which deserves special mention for ingenuity and charm, was erected in a small garden. An inspired and generous adult gave the children a meringue-shaped wedding dress to play with. Using clothes pegs, the children suspended the frothy white garment between the washing line and the bushes, creeping under the satin to play in secret bliss beneath the white lacy roof of their exotic pavilion.

It is easy for us to shatter the fragile dream of children's play. Our adult intrusions are often clumsy and insensitive, our belief in the pretend quickly exposed as fraudulent. Slow and cumbersome, with our feet of clay, we lack the quick wit to keep pace with the child's mind, and the magic slows and stops. Developing the tact and grace to collude in the conspiracy of children's fiction, '…taking care not to decimate it with adult carelessness. Or affection',[149] is something few of us manage to achieve. Those who do are not forgotten.

Sanctioning play with all its ramifications also means having faith in children, and accepting them as people who need to make mistakes and who must rely on our tolerance when they do so.

Russell Evans, author of *Helping Children to Overcome Fear*, recounts an incident which portrays a child's vulnerability, and – although too modest to admit it – his own remarkable tolerance and forgiveness in the face of the child's error.

Russell and his wife Jean, a hospital play therapist, always invited the local children to play in their garden. They performed puppet shows and had special festivals for their own and the neighbourhood children at Christmas and at other times. That particular summer, Russell was especially proud of the pair of newly installed glass sliding-door windows leading out to the back garden, which he had purchased at considerable cost. One day, he was in another part of the house when he heard a great smash, immediately followed by a splintering sound. His heart sank as he went to investigate. There in the garden, amidst the shards of broken glass, stood a small child holding the handle of a hammer without its head. 'I didn't mean to', he said. 'I was swinging the hammer round and round and the head flew off.' Russell, to his everlasting credit, didn't react in anger. He merely said, 'Never mind, it was an accident'. A moment or two later, the boy's older sister appeared. Horrified, at what she saw she said to Russell, 'Your window's smashed'. The boy looked at Russell, anticipating the sky to fall around him and his sister upon him; but what Russell calmly said, without even a glance at the poor, trembling culprit, was, 'Yes, it was an accident'.

At Christmas that year, everyone was invited to a candle-lit ceremony around the tree, where there were presents for everybody. The boy held out his hands to receive his present. It was an odd shape and strangely heavy. The boy unwrapped it and his sister said, 'Oh he's got a hammer, he loves playing around doing bits of woodwork and making things.' The boy, now a man, never forgot that gesture of faith and has remained in contact with Russell ever since.

The obituary of the judge and Lord Justice of Appeal Sir Roualeyn Cumming-Bruce (*The Times* 14/06/00), mentioned a similar incident from his childhood, an incident which proved deeply significant throughout his life. Described as a compassionate judge, Roualeyn the child was once forgiven by the Duchess of Devonshire for an unfortunate breakage. As a boy he had been taken for tea at Chatsworth House, where a game of hide and seek had ensued. He was lowered into one of a pair of rare, and extremely valuable, Chinese vases by two friends – a splendid hiding place for a small child! After waiting quite some time to be discovered, he realised he had been forgotten and wondered if he would ever be found. Too small to climb out, he rocked the vase to and fro until it toppled over. He escaped but was filled with shame at the sight of the broken vase. An honest child, he went to tell the Duchess of Devonshire what had happened and poured out the whole sad story to her. She responded with great compassion, forbearance and generosity by telling the little miscreant not to worry – she had another one just like it (a *pair* of matching vases!). She also said that he should tell no one about the mishap until he was 21 – this was because she knew that his father, an impoverished parson, would no doubt ruin himself in the effort to pay for the damage.

The generosity and compassion shown to the young boy by this enlightened woman is remarkable. One wonders how often the memory of how he had once been judged himself lent understanding, wisdom, and compassion to the way this 'compassionate' judge' meted out justice to others?

We all need adults who will love us and forgive us the faults we could not help by virtue of our being children. We know who understood us as children: we remember those adults who recognized us, who saw us, or who heard us; who asked: 'How can I give you the form you need and leave you free? What kind of space can we create around the child? Where is the space between repression and freedom? Can we strike a balance between forbidding and permitting?'

The future direction of children's play rests in our hands. Our human need to play is urgent and real. We need to stretch the wings of our imaginations and fly a little in our childhood: we are old for a long time. We need to remember, and notice what children need; what they are telling us. Perhaps we also need to slow down and give ourselves some time to play.

Nature in her wisdom gives the young a playful spirit. The genius of play helps children meet their futures; it prepares them for a changing world and engages them absolutely with the present. Let us honour childhood, and give our children time to play.

Childhood! Winged likenesses half-guessed at, wheeling,
oh where, oh, where?

Rainer Maria Rilke[150]

Footnotes

1 Quoted in *The Times*, 15 July 2000.
2 Cathy Nutbrown, 'Wide eyes and open minds', in Nutbrown (ed.), *Respectful Educators – Capable Learners*, Paul Chapman, London, 1996, p. 53.
3 Iona and Peter Opie, *Children's Games*, Oxford University Press, 1984 (orig. publ. 1969), p. 13.
4 Ibid., p. 14.
5 *The Times*, 5 August 1995.
6 R. S. Thomas, *Selected Poems 1946-1968*, Bloodaxe Books, UK, 1990.
7 J. Huizinga, *Homo Ludens: A Study of the Play Element in Culture*, Beacon Press, Boston, Mass., 1955, p. 19.
8 S. Millar, *The Psychology of Play*, Penguin Books, Harmondsworth, 1969, p. 17.
9 Ibid.
10 Ibid.
11 Tina Bruce, *Time to Play in Early Childhood Education*, Hodder & Stoughton, London, 1999, p. 33 (orig. publ. 1991).
12 Ibid., p. 32
13 Huizinga (see note 7), p. 37.
14 Ibid., p. 9.
15 Stuart Brown, *ReVision* (USA), 17 (4) (Spring), 1995.
16 Ibid.

17 Tina Bruce, *Early Childhood Education,* Hodder & Stoughton, London, 1995, p. 42. (orig. publ. 1987).

18 Edgar Klugman and Sara Smilansky, *Children's Play and Learning – Perspectives and Policy Implications,* Teachers College Press, New York, 1990, p. 19.

19 Ibid., p. 25.

20 Ibid., p. 26.

21 Bob Fagan, cited in Brown, *ReVision* (see note 15).

22 Smilansky, (see note 18), p. 26.

23 Ibid., p. 19.

24 Connolly and Doyle 1984, cited in Dorothy Faulkner's pamphlet *Play, Self and the Social World* – A Compilation of Writings on Play Theories prepared for the Michael Institute for Spatial Dynamics, p. 16.

25 Faulkner, p. 23 (see note 24).

26 Ibid., p. 24.

27 Vivian Gussin Paley, *The Kindness of Children,* Harvard University Press, Cambridge, Mass., 1999, p. 67.

28 Prosser et al. (1986), cited in A. Curtis 'Play in different cultures and childhoods', in J. Moyles (ed.), *The Excellence of Play,* Open University Press, Buckingham and Philadelphia, 1996 (orig. publ. in 1994), p. 30.

29 Henry Bett, *The Games of Children,* Methuen, London, 1929, p. 8.

30 Alice Bertha Gomme, *The Traditional Games of England, Scotland and Ireland,* Thames and Hudson, London, 1984 (orig. publ. in 1894), p. x.

31 Ibid., p. 111.

32 Ibid., p. 112.

33 Smilansky, p. 25 (see note 18).

34 Reidun Iverson, *The Child's World Upbringing and Education at the Pre-School Age,* (Translation), Edited by Arve Mathison, published in co-operation with the Executive Committee of the Steiner Kindergartens and Vidar Press, Norway, 1999, p. Q.

35 Tina Bruce, 'Play, the universe and everything!', in Moyles (ed.), *The Excellence of Play,* p. 196 (see note 28).

36 Reidun Iverson, p. Q (see note 34).

37 Rachel Carson, *The Sense of Wonder,* Harper and Collins, New York, 1998, p. 56.

38 George Eliot, *The Mill on the Floss,* Penguin Classics, Harmondsworth, 1985 (orig. publ. in 1880), p. 94.

39 Daniel Goleman, *Emotional Intelligence: Why it can Matter More than IQ,* Bloomsbury Publishing, London, 1996.

40 Janusz Korczak, *When I Am Little Again,* University Press of America, Maryland and London, 1992 (orig. publ. in 1925), p. 3. I am indebted to Mary Jane Drummond of the School of Education in Cambridge for introducing me to Korczak's work.

41 Margaret Lowenfeld, *Play in Childhood,* Gollancz, London, 1935, p. 17.

42 Dorothy and Jerome Singer, *The House of Make Believe,* Harvard University Press, Cambridge, Mass. and London, 1992 (orig. publ. in 1990), p. 108.

43 Ibid., p. 103.

44 Russell Evans, *Helping Children to Overcome Fear: The Healing Power of Play,* Hawthorn Press, Stroud, 2000.

45 Bruce, *Early Childhood Education,* p. 17 (see note 17).

46 Kathy Hunt, 'Respecting the wisdom of a young child in grief', in *Realising Children's Potential: Excellence in the Early Years, Conference Proceedings,* University of Newcastle Upon Tyne, 1999, p. 65.

47 Jane Hislam, 'Sex-differentiated play experiences and children's choices', in Moyles (ed.), *The Excellence of Play,* p. 42 (see note 28).

48 Lowenfeld, p. 324 (see note 41).

49 Smilansky, p. 176 (see note 18).

50 Goleman (see note 39).

51 Ibid., p. 98.

52 Ibid.

53 Huizinga, p. 162 (see note 7).

54 Bruce, *Time to Play in Early Childhood Education,* p. 117 (see note 11).

55 Goleman, p. 115 (see note 39).

56 Rudolf Steiner, *Man and the World of the Stars,* The Anthroposophic Press, New York, 1982 (original lectures given in 1922), p. 52.

57 Paley, p. 61 (see note 27).

58 Tower and Singer 'Imagination, Interest and Joy in Early Childhood' (1980), in David Cohen, *The Development of Play,* Routledge, London, 1993, p. 144.

59 T. S. Eliot, Burnt Norton, Four Quartets, *The Complete Poems and Plays of T. S. Eliot,* Faber & Faber, London, 1970.

60 Ted Hughes, *Selected Poems 1957-1981,* Faber & Faber, London, 1984.

61 F. Froebel, quoted in Lowenfeld, p. 30 (see note 41).

62 Rudolf Steiner, *The Renewal of Education through the Science of the Spirit,* Kolisko Archive Publications for the Steiner Waldorf Schools Fellowship, Forest Row, UK, 1981 (from lectures given in 1920), p. 169.

63 Ibid., p. 168.

64 See E. Lawrence, *The Origins and Growth of Modern Education,* Pelican, Harmondsworth, 1970, p. 244.

65 Seamus Heaney, *Opened Ground,* Faber & Faber, London, 1998.

66 Joseph Chilton Pearce, *The Magical Child,* Plume, New York, 1997, p. 95.

67 Meltzner, 1967, cited in Faulkner, p. 11 (see note 24).

68 James Hillman, *The Soul's Code: In Search of Character and Calling,* Bantam, London, 1997, p. 6.

69 R. L. Stephenson, from *Child's Play,* Scotland, 1881; cited in Michael Rosen (ed.), *The Penguin Book of Childhood,* Viking, London, 1994, p. 97.

70 J. Keats, to Benjamin Bailey, 22 November 1817.

71 Charles Dickens, quoted in *The Penguin Book of Childhood* (see note 69).

72 Singer and Singer, p. 19 (see note 42).

73 James Hillman, p. 46 (see note 68).

74 Ibid., p. 111.

75 Ibid., p.112.

76 William James, quoted in Hillman, p. 97 (see note 68).

77 Singer and Singer, p. 90 (see note 42).

78 Hillman, p. 112 (see note 68).

79 Bruno Bettelheim, *The Uses of Enchantment: The Meaning and Importance of Fairy Tales,* Penguin, Harmondsworth, 1976, p. 65.

80 M. J. Drummond, *Assessing Children's Learning,* David Fulton, London, 1993, p. 84

81 Ibid.

82 From Christine Levy, *Steiner Education,* Vol. 31, No. 1, 1997 (Steiner Schools Fellowship Publications, Forest Row, UK), p. 36.

83 Quoted in Bettelheim, p. 64 (see note 79).

84 Egan, cited in 'Play and legislated curriculum', Angela Anning, Moyles, p. 74 (see note 28).

85 Huizinga, p. 137 (see note 7).

86 Rainer Maria Rilke, 'The Sonnets to Orpheus', Second Part, *Rainer Maria Rilke: Selected Poems,* translated by J. B. Leishman, Penguin, Harmondsworth, 1964, orig. publ. in German in 1922.

87 Pearce, p. 117 (see note 66).

88 Singer and Singer, p. 194 (see note 42).

89 Ibid.

90 Ibid., p. 278.

91 Ibid., p. 177.

92 Marie Winn, *The Plug-in Drug,* Penguin, New York and London, 1985 (orig. publ. in 1977), p. 10.

93 David Cohen (see note 58), p. 109.

94 Singer and Singer, (see note 42), p. 91.
95 Samuel Taylor Coleridge, *Biographia Literaria,* Ch. 13.
96 Howard Gardner, cited in Eugene Schwartz, 'ADHD – a challenge of our times', *Waldorf Education Research Bulletin,* Vol. IV, No. I (January), New York 1999, p. 11.
97 Pearce, p. 117 (see note 66).
98 George Eisen, *Children at Play in the Holocaust: Games among the Shadows,* University of Massachusetts Press, 1990 (orig. publ. in 1943), p. 72.
99 Mary Jane Drummond, *Play, Learning and the National Curriculum* in T. Cox (ed) *The National Curriculum and the Early Years,* Falmer, London, 1996.
100 Singer and Singer, p. 231 (see note 42).
101 Padraic Colum, introduction to *Grimms Fairy Tales,* Routledge and Kegan Paul, London, 1975, p. ix.
102 Sally Jenkinson, quoted in Marian Whitehead, *Supporting Language and Literacy Developments in the Early Years,* Open University Press, Buckingham, 1999, p. 89.
103 Huizinga, p. 119 (see note 7).
104 Ibid., p. 134.
105 Jenkinson, p. 89 (see note 102).
106 David Elkind, *Miseducation: Pre-Schoolers at Risk,* Alfred A. Knopf, New York, 1987, p. 122.
107 Birgitta Olafson, quoted in Iverson, p. L (see note 34).
108 Terry Brazelton, cited in Elkind, p. 8 (see note 106).
109 Libby Purves, *The Times,* 15 June 1999.
110 T. S. Eliot, Choruses from the Rock, in *The Complete Poems and Plays of T. S. Eliot,* Faber & Faber, London, 1970.
111 Elkind, quoted in E. Ogletree *School Readiness: The Developmental View,* Steiner Education Monograph, Steiner Waldorf Schools Fellowship, Forest Row, UK, 1997, p. 41.
112 Jon Roar, with thanks to Jeichen Stapel, Reggio Emilia Educator – International Schools' Conference, Aberdeen (UK), 1999.

[113] H. Britz-Crecelius, *Children at Play: Preparation for Life,* Floris Books, Edinburgh, 1972, p. 69.

[114] *The Big Picture: Bright Futures,* Mental Health Foundation (20-21 Cornwall Terrace, London NW1 4LQ), 1999.

[115] Struck P. *Waldorf Education Research Bulletin,* Volume IV No 1 (January), New York 1999, p31.

[116] Winn, p. 10 (see note 92).

[117] Roy Porter, reviewing Susan Greenfield's *The Private Life of the Brain, The Times,* 14 June 2000.

[118] D. Webb, in A. Gomme, *The Traditional Games of England, Scotland and Ireland,* Thames and Hudson, London, 1984, p. 15.

[119] Ibid.

[120] Neil Postman, *The Disappearance of Childhood,* W. H. Allen, London,1983, p. 79.

[121] Opie and Opie, p. 14 (see note 3).

[122] Quoted in *The Times,* 3 July 2000.

[123] Mary Brown, quoted in S. Humphries, J. Mack and R. Perks, *A Century of Childhood,* Sidgwick & Jackson, London, 1988, p. 67.

[124] Ibid., p. 79.

[125] Cohen, p. 63 (see note 58).

[126] Piaget, cited in Cohen, p. 4 (see note 58).

[127] Singer and Singer, p. 84 (see note 42).

[128] Quoted in an article by W. Langley and S. Patten in *The Times,* 6 July 2000.

[129] Hyman, Chairman of Verdict retail consultancy group, quoted in ibid.

[130] Langley and Patten (ibid.).

[131] A. Curtis, cited in Moyles (ed.), p. 31 (see note 28).

[132] Winifred Foley, *Child in the Forest,* BBC, London (undated), p. 18.

[133] *Times Educational Supplement,* 10 May 1996.

[134] Humphries et al, *A Century of Childhood*, p. 62 (see note 123).

[135] David Roberts, 'Toys aren't us' (Letter), *The Independent*, Education Supplement, 18 November 1999, p. 6.

[136] Lerner and Sylva both quoted in 'Children play less the more toys they get', *Sunday Times*, 25 February 2001.

[137] Quoted in A. Schorsch, *Images of Childhood: An Illustrated Social History*, Mayflower Books, New York, 1979, p. 101.

[138] Elizabeth Stutz, 'Violent electronic entertainment: its effects on the development of children and the implications for world peace, and some possible steps to reverse the trend', paper published by 'Play for Life' (4 Guildhall Hill, Norwich, Norfolk NR2 1JH, UK).

[139] Sally Jenkinson, 'As ye sow so shall ye reap', in *Paedeia: A Research Journal for Waldorf Education*, Issue 17 (Steiner Waldorf Schools Fellowship, Forest Row, UK), p. 52.

[140] Lowenfeld, p. 16 (see note 41).

[141] James Hillman, p. 100 (see note 68).

[142] Rudolf Steiner, *The Education of the Child*, Anthroposophic Press, Hudson, NY, 1996, p. 87.

[143] Ibid., p. 97.

[144] Cathy Nutbrown, *Threads of Thinking – young children learning and the role of early education*, PCP/SAGE, London, 1999.

[145] Abbey National Bank, UK, reported in *The Times* newspaper, 31 August 1999.

[146] Ibid.

[147] David Elkind, quoted in E. Klugman and S. Smilansky (eds), *Children's Play and Learning*, Teachers College Press, New York and London, 1990, p. 11.

[148] Singer and Singer, p. 4 (see note 42).

[149] Arundhati Roy, *The God of Small Things*, Flamingo, London, 1998, p. 190.

[150] Rainer Maria Rilke, 'Childhood', in *Selected Poems*, (see note 86).

Bibliography

BALL, Sir C. (1994) *Start Right*, Royal Society of Arts, London

BERGER, J. (1977) *Ways of Seeing*, Penguin and the BBC, London (orig. publ. in 1972)

BETT, H. (1929) *The Games of Children*, Methuen, London

BETTELHEIM, B. (1991) *The Uses of Enchantment: The Meaning and Importance of Fairy Tales*, Penguin, Harmondsworth, (orig. publ. in 1976)

BIDDULPH, S. (1998) *Raising Boys*, Thorsons, London, (orig. publ. in 1997)

BLAKE, W. (1967) *Songs of Innocence and Experience*, Rupert Hart-Davis Ltd., London in association with the Trianon Press, Paris

BRITZ-CRECELIUS, H. (1972) *Children at Play – Preparation for Life*, Floris Books, Edinburgh

BRUCE, T. (1999) *Time to Play in Early Childhood Education*, Hodder & Stoughton, London, (orig. publ. in 1991)

BRUCE, T. (1995) *Early Childhood Education*, Hodder & Stoughton, London, (orig. publ. in 1987)

CARSON, R. (1998) *The Sense of Wonder*, Harper and Collins, New York

COHEN, D. (1993) *The Development of Play*, Routledge, London (orig. publ. in 1987)

COX, T. (ed.) (1996) *The National Curriculum and the Early Years*, Falmer, London

DRUMMOND M. J. (1993) *Assessing Children's Learning*, David

Fulton, London

EGAN, K. (1997) *The Educated Mind,* University of Chicago Press, Chicago

EISEN, G. (1990) *Children at Play in the Holocaust: Games among the Shadows,* University of Massachusetts Press, (orig. publ. in 1943)

ELIOT, G. (1985) *The Mill on the Floss,* Penguin Classics, Harmondsworth, London (orig. publ. in 1880)

ELIOT, T. S. (1970) *The Complete Poems and Plays of T.S. Eliot,* Faber & Faber, London

ELKIND, D. (1981) *The Hurried Child: Growing up Too Fast Too Soon,* Addison-Wesley, Reading, Mass.

ELKIND, D. (1997) *Miseducation: Pre-Schoolers at Risk,* Knopf, New York (orig. publ. in 1987)

EVANS, R. (2000) *Helping Children to Overcome Fear: The Healing Power of Play,* Hawthorn Press, Stroud

FOLEY, W. *Child in the Forest,* BBC, London (undated)

FROMM, E. (1997) *To Have or to Be,* Abacus, London (orig. publ. in 1976)

GOLDING, W. (1972) *Lord of the Flies,* Faber & Faber, London.

GOLEMAN, D. (1996) *Emotional Intelligence: Why It Can Matter More Than IQ,* Bloomsbury, London

GOMME, A. (1984) *The Traditional Games of England, Scotland and Ireland,* Thames and Hudson, London

GRIMM, J. & W. (1975) *Grimm's Fairy Tales,* Routledge and Kegan Paul, London (orig. publ. in UK in 1853)

HEANEY, S. (1998) *Opened Ground,* Faber & Faber, London

HILLMAN, J. (1997) *The Soul's Code: In Search of Character and Calling,* Bantam, London

HUGHES, T. (1998) *Selected Poems 1957-1981,* Faber & Faber, London

HUIZINGA, J. (1955) *Homo Ludens: A Study of the Play Element in Culture,* Beacon Press, Boston, Mass.

HUMPHRIES, S., MACK, J. & PERKS, R. (1988) *A Century of*

Childhood, Sidgwick & Jackson, London

HUNT, K. (1999) 'Respecting the Wisdom of the Young Child in Grief' in *Realising Children's Potential: Excellence in the Early Years,* Conference Proceedings, University of Newcastle Upon Tyne

KLUGMAN, E. and SMILANSKY, S. (1990) *Children's Play and Learning – Perspectives and Policy Implications,* Teachers College Press, New York

KORCZAK, J. (1992) *When I Am Little Again,* University Press of America, Maryland and London (orig. publ. in 1925)

LAWRENCE, E. (1970) *The Origins and Growth of Modern Education,* Pelican, Harmondsworth

LOWENFELD, M. (1935) *Play in Childhood,* Victor Gollancz, London

MARKS, E. (1997) *Observations of Children* (unpublished mimeo)

MATHISON, A. (1999) *The Child's World: Upbringing and Education at Preschool Age,* in co-operation with the Executive Committee of the Steiner Kindergartens, and Vidar Publishing, Norway

MILLAR, S. (1969) *The Psychology of Play,* Penguin Books, Harmondsworth

MOYLES, J. (ed.) (1996) *The Excellence of Play,* Open University Press, Buckingham and Philadelphia (orig. publ. in 1994)

NUTBROWN, C. (ed.) (1996) *Respectful Educators – Capable Learners,* Paul Chapman, London

NUTBROWN, C. (1999) *Threads of Thinking – young children learning and the role of early education,* London: PCP/SAGE

OPIE, I. & P. (1984) *Children's Games,* Oxford University Press, Oxford (orig. publ. 1969)

PALEY, V. GUSSIN (1999) *The Kindness of Children,* Harvard University Press, Cambridge, Mass.

PEARCE, J. C. (1997) *The Magical Child,* Plume, New York

POSTMAN, N. (1983) *The Disappearance of Childhood,* W. H. Allen, London

RILKE, R. M. (1964) 'Childhood', in *Selected Poems,* translated by J. B. Leishman, Penguin, Harmondsworth (orig. publ. in German in 1922).

ROSEN, M. (1994) *The Penguin Book of Childhood,* Viking, London

ROUSSEAU, J. J. (1991) *Emile,* Dent, London (orig. publ. in 1762)

ROY, A. (1998) *The God of Small Things,* Flamingo, London

SCHORSCH, A. (1979) I*mages of Childhood: An Illustrated Social History,* Mayflower Books, USA

SINGER, D. G. & SINGER J. L. (1992) *The House of Make Believe,* Harvard University Press, Cambridge, Mass. and London (orig. publ. in 1990)

STEINER, R. (1981) *The Renewal of Education through the Science of the Spirit,* Kolisko Archive Publications for the Steiner Waldorf Schools Fellowship, Forest Row, UK (from lectures given in 1920)

STEINER, R. (1982) *Man and the World of the Stars,* Anthroposophic Press, New York (lectures given in 1922)

STEINER, R. (1988) *The Gospel of St Luke,* Rudolf Steiner Press, London (orig. publ. in 1909)

STEINER, R. (1995) *The Education of the Child in the Light of Anthroposophy,* Rudolf Steiner Publishing Co., London

STEINER, R. (1996) *The Education of the Child,* Anthroposophic Press, New York (orig. publ. in 1907)

STUTZ, E. (1995) 'Violent electronic entertainment: its effects on the development of children and the implications for world peace and some possible steps to reverse the trend,' Play for Life, Norwich

THOMAS, R. S. (1990) *Selected Poems 1946-1968,* Bloodaxe Books, UK

WHITEHEAD, M. (1999) Supporting Language and Literacy Development in the Early Years, Open University Press, Buckingham

WINN, M. (1985) *The Plug-in Drug,* Penguin, New York and London (orig. publ. in 1977)

Appendix 1:
IPA Declaration of the Child's Right to Play

International Association for the Child's Right to Play

WHAT IS PLAY?

CHILDREN are the foundation of the world's future.

CHILDREN have played at all times throughout history and in all cultures.

PLAY, along with the basic needs of nutrition, health, shelter and education, is vital to develop the potential of all children.

PLAY is communication and expression, combining thought and action; it gives satisfaction and a feeling of achievement.

PLAY is instinctive, voluntary, and spontaneous.

PLAY helps children develop physically, mentally, emotionally and socially.

PLAY is a means of learning to live, not a mere passing of time.

ALARMING TRENDS AFFECTING CHILDHOOD

IPA is deeply concerned by a number of alarming trends and their negative impact on children's development:

- Society's indifference to the importance of play
- Over-emphasis on theoretical and academic studies in schools.
- Increasing numbers of children living with inadequate provisions for survival and development.
- Inadequate environmental planning, which results in a lack of basic amenities, inappropriate housing forms, and poor traffic management.
- Increasing commercial exploitation of children, and the deterioration of cultural traditions.
- Lack of access for third world women to basic training in childcare and development.
- Inadequate preparation of children to cope with life in a rapidly changing society.
- Increasing segregation of children in the community.
- The increasing numbers of working children, and their unacceptable working conditions.
- Constant exposure of children to war, violence, exploitation and destruction.
- Over-emphasis on unhealthy competition and "winning at all costs" in children's sports.

PROPOSALS FOR ACTION

The following proposals are listed under the names of government departments having a measure of responsibility for children.

HEALTH
Play is essential for the physical and mental health of the child.

- Establish programmes for professionals and parents about the benefits of play from birth onwards.
- Ensure basic conditions (nutrition, sanitation, clean water and air) which promote the healthy survival and development of all children.
- Incorporate play into community programmes designed to maintain children's physical and mental health.
- Include play as an integral part of all children's environments, including hospitals and other institutional settings.

EDUCATION
Play is part of education.

- Provide opportunities for initiative, interaction, creativity and socialisation through play in formal education systems.
- Include studies of the importance of play and the means of play provision in the training of all professionals and volunteers working with and for children.
- Strengthen play provision in primary schools to enhance learning and to maintain attendance and motivation.
- Reduce the incompatibilities between daily life, work and education by involving schools and colleges, and by using public buildings for community play programmes.
- Ensure that working children have access to play and learning opportunities outside of the system of formal education.

WELFARE
Play is an essential part of family and community life.

- Ensure that play is accepted as an integral part of social development and social care.
- Promote measures that strengthen positive relationships between parents and children.
- Ensure that play is part of community-based services designed to integrate children with physical, mental or emotional disabilities into the community.
- Provide safe play environments that protect children against abduction, sexual abuse and physical violence.

LEISURE
Children need opportunities to play at leisure.

- Provide time, space, materials, natural settings, and programmes with leaders where children may develop a sense of belonging, self-esteem, and enjoyment through play.
- Enable interaction between children and people of all backgrounds and ages in leisure settings.
- Encourage the conservation and use of traditional indigenous games.
- Stop the commercial exploitation of children's play, and the production and sale of war toys and games of violence and destruction.
- Promote the use of co-operative games and fair play for children in sports.
- Provide all children, particularly those with special needs, with access to a diversity of play environments, toys and play materials through community programmes such as pre-school play groups, toy libraries and play buses.

PLANNING
The needs of the child must have priority in the planning of human settlements.

- Ensure that children and young people can participate in making decisions that affect their surroundings and their access to them.
- When planning new, or reorganising existing developments, recognise the child's small size and limited range of activity.
- Disseminate existing knowledge about play facilities and play programmes to planning professionals and politicians.
- Oppose the building of high-rise housing and provide opportunities to mitigate its detrimental effects on children and families.
- Enable children to move easily about the community by providing safe pedestrian access through urban neighborhoods, better traffic management, and improved public transportation.
- Increase awareness of the high vulnerability of children living in slum settlements, tenements, and derelict neighborhoods.
- Reserve adequate and appropriate space for play and recreation through statutory provision.

The IPA Declaration of the Child's Right to Play was originally produced in November 1977 at the IPA Malta Consultation held in preparation for the International Year of the Child (1979). It was revised by the IPA International Council in Vienna, September 1982, and Barcelona, September 1989.

The IPA Declaration should be read in conjunction with Article 31 of the United Nations Convention on the Rights of the Child (adopted by the UN General Assembly on November 20, 1989), which states that the child has a right to leisure, play, and participation in cultural and artistic activities.

Appendix 2:
Television as a Public Health Issue

Numerous studies have raised serious concerns about the impact of excessive television watching on human development and behavior, especially among young children. Excessive television watching is a prime culprit in some of today's leading health epidemics; aggressive behavior, depression, sedentariness, obesity and heart disease. Lack of exercise and a poor diet, to which TV-watching is fundamentally linked, is the second leading cause of death (behind tobacco) in the U.S. The American medical community has long spoken out about the need to reduce TV watching and takes an activist stance with its endorsement/support of National TV-Turnoff Week. Issues of concern among health care professionals include the following:

Obesity/Sedentariness: Thirty-three percent of all adults and 11percent of today's children are overweight,[1] raising their risk of illnesses such as heart disease, high blood pressure, diabetes and colon cancer. The cause of this obesity epidemic: inactivity and a high-calorie diet. And a primary accomplice is excessive television watching. In March 1998 the *Journal of the American Medical Association* confirmed that children who watch four or more hours of television/day are significantly heavier than children who watch less than two hours/day.

Inactivity: The 1996 *Surgeon General's Report on Physical Activity and Health* showed that 60 percent of Americans don't get enough physical exercise to stay healthy, and 25 percent engage in no physical activity whatsoever. The average American spends 40 percent of his/her leisure time watching TV.[2] According to obesity expert Dr. William Dietz, Director of the Division of Nutrition and Physical Activity at the Centers for Disease Control, 'The easiest way to reduce inactivity is to turn off the TV set. Almost anything else uses more energy than watching TV.'

High-Calorie Diet: Television commercials promote a high fat, high sugar and high salt diet. A 1991 study documented 202 ads for junk food such as sugared cereals, candy and chips during four hour of Saturday- morning cartoons.[3] The dietary advice of most television commercials is extremely unhealthy and clearly contradicts nutrition guidelines recommended by the U.S. Departments of Agriculture, Health and Human Services and the U.S. Surgeon General.

In addition to promoting an unhealthy diet, television creates an environment that is conducive to eating. Many children and adults tend to snack while watching TV. A positive correlation between television viewing by children and: 1) between-meal snacking, 2) consumption of foods advertised on television and 3) children's attempts to influence their parent's food purchases has been clearly documented.[4]

Violence/Aggressive Behavior: Today the average child watches 8,000 murders on TV before finishing elementary school. By age eighteen, the average American has seen 200,000 acts of violence on TV, including 16,000 murders.[5] The 1998 National Television Violence Study (paid for by the National Cable Television Association) found that 67 percent of prime time programs on broadcast networks (and 64 percent of basic cable programs) contained violence, a 12 percent increase since 1994. Ninety-two percent of premium cable shows contain violence.

Young children are unable to distinguish fantasy from reality and often accept cruel and aggressive television scenes as real and normal. Today, particularly among children and adolescents, aggressive behavior is all too often a first, not a last, response to interpersonal conflict.[6] Primary concerns regarding television violence include:

Increased Aggressive Behavior: Infants as young as fourteen months have been show to imitate violent behavior seen on television including cartoons and slapstick violence.[7] Aggressive behavior learned at an early age may be difficult to unlearn. In a 22-year old longitudinal study, Drs. Eron and Huessman at the University of Michigan concluded that violent television watched in childhood correlated positively with subsequent aggressive behavior as an adult.[8]

Desensitization: Children who repeatedly view violent acts on television become 'desensitized' and are less likely to respond appropriately to real-life violence or victims of attacks. Adults may also show symptoms of desensitization; for example, the American Medical Association reports that men can become less sensitive to domestic violence victims after watching violent tapes.[9] Desensitization can also increase a viewer's appetite for violence.

Mean World Syndrome: Because television is so filled with violent imagery, heavy TV viewers tend to believe the world (and their community) is a far more dangerous place than do light viewers. Dr George Gerbner of the Annenberg School of Communication, calls this effect the 'Mean World Syndrome'. The more violence one sees on television, the more anxious and threatened one feels. As a result we become more willing to depend on authorities, strong measures, gated communities, and other proto-police-state accoutrements.[10]

Television Dependence: Millions of Americans are so hooked on television that they fit the criteria for substance dependence as defined by the official psychiatric manual. According to Rutgers University psychologist, Robert Kubey, heavy TV viewers exhibit five dependency symptoms – two more than are necessary to arrive at a clinical diagnosis of substance abuse.[11] These include:

- While intending to watch only a program or two, most TV viewers end up watching hour after hour;
- Even those who recognise that they watch too much television don't seem able to cut down;
- Important family or personal activities get cancelled or reduced to fit in with television;
- Viewers find it more difficult to turn the television off the longer they view;
- Withdrawal symptoms set in when heavy viewers stop or cut back their tube time.

Sexual Attitude and Behavior: American television is extremely sexually suggestive: the average American teenage views over 14,000 sexual references annually. In the absence of effective education at home and school, television has become the leading sex educator in American today, yet television actors rarely mention abstinence, birth control, or sexually transmitted diseases. The message more typically reflects a 'just do it' attitude. Dr. Mary Pipher, psychologist and author of *Reviving Ophelia*, writes: 'The Hollywood model of sexual behavior couldn't be more harmful and misleading if it were trying to be.' Several studies have demonstrated a link between television programs and changes in teenagers' behavior and attitudes.[12]

- In a study of 75 adolescent girls, half of whom were pregnant, the pregnant girls watched more soap operas before becoming pregnant and were less likely to think that their favorite soap characters would use birth control.[13]

- A study of 326 Cleveland teenagers showed that those with a preference for MTV had increased amount of sexual experience in their mid-teen years.[14]
- A 1997 study found that young teenagers exposed to more soap operas and talk shows tended to have beliefs consistent with what they were viewing (e.g. 'married people often cheat on their husband or wife', 'most of my friends have had sex with someone').[15]

Eating Disorders: Today, television actresses are 23 percent thinner than the average woman. Television promotes a stereotypical ultra-slender female body image while subjecting viewers to commercials for high-fat, high-sugar foods. The result is a mixed message of 'thin is in' and 'eat, eat, eat.' An adaptive response to this contradiction may be the practice of bingeing and purging known as bulimia, which enables one to eat excessively and remain thin. An estimated 3 to 10 percent of adolescent and college-aged women are bulimic. Bulimia can lead to some serious health consequences including dental problems, esophageal tears, gastro-intestinal problems and electrolytic imbalances that can trigger heart attacks.[16]

Alcohol Abuse: A 1998 Stanford University study found that teens who watch more television and music videos are significantly more likely to start drinking alcohol. Alcohol is involved in 25-50% of all adolescent deaths.[17] Young people typically begin drinking alcohol in early adolescence: by the time they graduate from high school, two-thirds have become regular drinkers, and two-fifths exhibit frequent binge drinking.[18] American youths view between 1,000 and 2,000 beer and liquor commercials per year, and many of the implicit messages are meant to appeal specifically to them: alcohol is fun, people who drink alcohol are more sophisticated, sexy, and 'real' men drink beer.[19] Alcohol manufacturers spend

$900 million a year for advertising, and US per capital consumption of alcohol has increased 50 percent since 1960.

References

1   National Center for Health Statistics, Center for Disease Control and Prevention
2   *Wall Street Journal,* November 20, 1996
3   Center for Science in the Public Interest Report, 1991
4   Dietz WH, Gortmaker SL, 'Do we fatten our children at the television set? Obesity and television viewing in children and adolescents', *Pediatrics* 75: 807-812, 1985
5   *Physicians Guide to Media Violence,* American Medical Association
6   Levine M, 'TV violence and our children', *Washington Times,* Aug. 9, 1996
7   Centerwall B, 'Television and Violence', JAMA 267: 3059-3063, 1992
8   Huessman LD, Eron LD, Klein R et. al. 'The stability of aggression over time and generations', Dev. Psychol 20: 1120-1134, 1984
9   *Physician's Guide to Media Violence,* American Medical Association
10 Stossel S, *The Man Who Counts the Killing,* Atlantic Monthly May 1997
11 MacBeth T, *Tuning in to Young Viewers,* pp 227-232, Sage Publications 1996
12 Strasburger V, 'Sex, Drugs, Rock 'n' Roll' and the media – Are the media responsible for adolescent behavior?' Adolescent Medicine: State of the Art Reviews, 8: 403-413, 1997
13 Corder-Bolz C, 'Television and adolescents' sexual behavior' Sex Education Coalition News 3:40, 1981
14 Peterson JL, Moore KA, 'Media preferences of sexually active teens'. Presented at the annual meeting of the American Psychological Association, Toronto, August 26, 1984

15 Strasburger VC, Furno-Lamude D, 'The effects of media consumption on adolescents' sexual attitudes and practices. Results of a pilot study' (manuscript)

16 Dietz W, 'Television, obesity and eating disorders', Adolescent Medicine: State of the Art Reviews, 4: 543-548, 1993

17 Robinson T, Chen H, Television and music video exposure and risk of adolescent alcohol use, Pediatrics Vol. 102 No. 5, 1998

18 Atkin C, Effects of Media Alcohol Messages on Adolescent Audiences Adolescent Medicine State of the Art Reviews 4: 527-542, 1993

19 Strasburger V, 'Children, Adolescents, and the Media: Five Crucial Issues', Adolescent Medicine: State of the Art Reviews 4|: 479-493, 1993

Appendix 3:
Television Statistics

According to the A.C Nielson Co. (1998), the average American watches 3 hours and 46 minutes of TV each day(more than 52 days of nonstop TV-watching per year). **By age 65 the average American will have spent nearly 9 years glued to the tube.**

A. Family Life

1. Percentage of US households with at least one television: 98
2. Percentage of US households with at least one VCR: 84
3. Percentage of US households with two TV sets: 34;
   three or more TV sets: 40
4. Hours per day that TV is on in an average US home: 7 hours, 12 minutes
5. Percentage of Americans that regularly watch television while eating dinner: 66
6. Number of videos rented daily in the US: 6 million
7. Number of public library items checked out daily: 3 million
8. Chance that an American falls asleep with the TV on at least three nights a week: 1 in 4
9. Percentage of Americans who say they watch too much TV: 49

B. Childhood and Education

1. Number of minutes per week that the average American child ages 2-11 watches television: 1,197
2. Number of minutes per week that parents spend in meaningful conversation with their children: 38.5
3. Percentage of children ages 5-17 who have a TV in their bedroom: 52
4. Percentage of children ages 2-5 who have a TV in their bedroom: 25

5. Percentage of day care centres that use TV during a typical day: 70
6. Percentage of parents who would like to limit their children's TV watching: 73
7. Percentage of 4-6 year olds who, when asked to choose between watching TV and spending time with their fathers, preferred television: 54
8. Hours per week of TV watching shown to negatively affect academic achievement: 10 or more
9. Percentage of 4th graders that watch more than 14 hours of television per week: 81
10. Hours per year the average American youth watches television: 1,500
11. Hours per year the average American youth spends in school: 900
12. Chance that an American parent requires that children do their homework before watching TV: 1 in 12
13. Percentage of teenagers 13-17 who can name the city where the US Constitution was written (Philadelphia): 25
14. Percentage of teenagers 13-17 who can know where you find the zip code (Beverly Hills): 75

C. Violence and Health

1. Number of violent acts the average American child sees on TV by age 18: 200,000
2. Number of murders witnessed by children on television by the age 18: 16,000
3. Percentage of Hollywood executives who believe there is a link between TV violence and real-life violence: 80
4. Percentage of children polled who said they felt 'upset' or 'scared' by violence on television: 91
5. Percent increase in network news coverage of homicide between 1990 and 1995: 336
6. Number of medical studies since 1985 linking excessive television watching to increasing rates of obesity: 12
7. Percentage of American children ages 6 to 11 who were seriously

overweight in 1963: 4.5; in 1993: 14.0

8. Number of ads aired for 'junk food' during four hours of Saturday morning cartoons: 202

D. Commercialism

1. Number of TV commercials seen in a year by an average child: 30,000
2. Number of TV commercials seen by the average American by age 65: 2 million
3. Percentage of toy advertising dollars spent on television commercials in 1997: 92
4. Percentage of Americans who believe that 'most of us buy and consume far more that we need': 82

E. General

1. Percentage of local TV news broadcast time devoted to advertising: 30
2. Percentage devoted to stories about crime, disaster and war: 53.8
3. Percentage devoted to public service announcements: 0.7
4. Total amount candidates spent on television ads during the 1996 political campaigns; $2.5 billion
5. Percentage of Americans who can name The Three Stooges: 59
6. Percentage of Americans who can name three Supreme Court Justices: 17

Compiled by TV-Turnoff Network: www. tvturnoff.org

Appendix 4:
Break Free of TV

Year round ideas to Break Free of TV!

1. Move the television set(s) to a less prominent location in the household. TV is far less tempting when it is not accessible.
2. Remove the TV set from your child's bedroom. A television in the bedroom draws children away from family activities and distracts them from homework, thinking, reading and sleeping. In addition, parents may find it difficult to monitor programs that are inappropriate or unhealthy.
3. Keep the TV off during dinner. Meals are a great time for conversation.
4. Place clear limits on television viewing. Try to restrict viewing to a half-hour per day or one hour every other evening. Explain your rules in positive, concrete terms. Try replacing 'You can't watch TV' with 'Let's turn off the TV so we can...'
5. Avoid using TV as a babysitter. Involve children in household activities and meal preparation. Make laundry folding into a game. Give them an opportunity to help out.
6. Designate certain days of the week as TV-free days (e.g. school nights).
7. Don't use TV as a reward or punishment. This increases its power and can lead to conflict over its use.
8. Listen to your favourite music or the radio instead of using TV as background noise.
9. Cancel your cable subscription. Use the monthly savings to buy a game or good book.
10. Don't let the TV displace what's important: family conversation, exercise, play, reading, creating, thinking and doing.

11. Consider living without television. Once you're TV-free you'll wonder how you ever had time to watch so much.

Source: TV-Turnoff Network www.tvturnoff.org

Beyond TV-Turnoff Week: Following up with Media Literacy

Television screens are packed with images that promote aggressive behavior, intolerance, risky sexual attitudes, alcohol consumption, excessive consumerism, unhealthy diets and gender/racial stereotypes. **Media literacy** is an important discipline that provides tools for analyzing, evaluating and criticizing these often harmful messages. Media literacy also involves learning how to control and reduce TV-watching – and taking an extended break away from television is a great first step. One especially effective media literacy curriculum has been developed by the New Mexico Media Literacy Project. A partial list of their recommendations follows.

1. **Provide better alternatives to TV.** Hundreds of activities are healthier for the family. You should have more fun playing with your children than watching television.
2. **Develop strict limits** for – or eliminate – passive screen time (TV, videos, computer games). The American Academy of Pediatrics recommends that children under two watch *no* television at all.
3. **Censor media** that run counter to your values or are developmentally inappropriate. Many programs and commercials, especially those with violent or sexual content, are simply not suitable for children.
4. **Learn advertisers' techniques of manipulation.** Until age nine or ten, children are often unaware that media is designed to sell products. Help them understand that commercials frequently

make toys appear more exciting than they really are and that the sugary foods and caffeinated drinks advertised may not be healthy.

5. **Investigate the media attitudes** of baby-sitters, daycare centers and other caregivers. Avoid those that use television to keep children occupied.

6. **Learn media issues** and discuss them when your child is old enough. Explain how TV programs often reduce complex problems to simple solutions. Children need to understand the real consequences and suffering caused by violence. Talk to them about non-aggressive solutions to conflict. As appropriate, teach older children and teenagers to analyze harmful messages such as gender stereotyping, glamorization of alcohol and tobacco use and risky sexual attitudes.

7. **Insist that children be critical.** Ask them questions. Television is a strange and powerful teacher that frequently teaches unhealthy lessons. Don't let passive acceptance become a habit.

8. **View programs on tape.** This allows the program to be stopped for discussion and the commercials to be fast forwarded.

9. **Discussion is not always a panacea.** Many well-intended parents forget to discuss programs or discuss them so superficially that the child does not benefit. Television is a powerful, multi-sensory teacher of values. Even under the best circumstances, it can be difficult for parents to be as persuasive. The off switch is always an option.

10. **Do not be misled by TV industry-sponsored 'media literacy' groups.** Family discussion and analysis of media are important, but some 'media literacy' groups over-emphasize the value of critical viewing and discussion without mentioning the importance of watching less. These *Astroturf* (as opposed to grassroots) groups are generally sponsored by large television and media conglomerates. The last thing these companies want is for kids to watch less TV, yet that may be the most important part of media literacy.

11. **Most of all, engage your children.** Read, talk, play and create with them. Give children a sense of pride in family discussions. This will translate into more accomplishment, healthier relationships, better grades and genuine self-esteem. Don't let television displace that which is crucial for your child's development.

Bob McCannon of the New Mexico Media Literacy Project contributed to this article.

For more information see www.nmmlp.org.

101 Screen-Free Activities

Activities for all ages

1. Learn to play a musical instrument.
2. Attend a community concert. Listen to a local band.
3. Organize a community clean-up or volunteer for a charity.
4. Visit the library. Borrow a book.
5. Go rollar skating, rollar blading or ice skating.
6. Listen to the radio.
7. Write an article, story, or poem.
8. Paint a picture, a mural or a room.
9. Visit a local bookstore.
10. Learn about native trees and flowers in your area. Plant something.
11. Write a letter to the President/Prime Minister, or your Representative and/or Senators or Member of Parliament.
12. Visit the zoo.
13. Go swimming. Join a community swim team
14. Read a book. Read to someone else.
15. Plan a picnic or barbecue.
16. Go bird watching. Learn the names of local birds.
17. Learn to change the oil or a tire on a car. Fix something.
18. Walk the dog. Wash the dog.

19. Visit the countryside. Visit the city. Travel by bus or train.
20. Write a letter to a friend or relative.
21. Bake cookies and bread. Make homemade jam. Share with a neighbour.
22. Plant a garden. Work in your garden.
23. Read magazines or newspapers. Swap them with friends.
24. Become a tutor.
25. Join a choir. Sing.
26. Go through your closets and clothes. Donate surplus items to charity or for recycling.
27. Start a diary/journal.
28. Go to a museum.
29. Take a nature hike.
30. Play cards.
31. Start a community exercise group that walks, runs or bikes.
32. Attend a religious service.
33. Feed fish or birds.
34. Make crafts to give as gifts. Try a new craft.
35. Do a crossword puzzle.
36. Watch the night sky through binoculars; identify different constellations. Observe the moon.[1]
37. Walk to work or school.
38. Start a bowling league.
39. Save money – cancel your cable TV!
40. Learn to use a compass.
41. Organize games such as football or baseball at the local park.
42. Learn about a different culture. Have an international dinner party.
43. Go for a bicycle ride.
44. Teach a child some of your favourite childhood games.
45. Learn yoga.
46. Take photographs. Organize photos into an album,
47. Study sign-language.
48. Play soccer, softball or volleyball.
49. Write a letter to your favourite author.

50. Visit and get to know your neighbours.
51. Cook dinner with friends or family.
52. Attend a live sports event.
53. Play frisbee.
54. Make cards for the holidays or birthdays.
55. Play chess, bridge or checkers.
56. Start a fiction book group. Start a public policy book group.
57. Go camping.
58. Take an early morning walk.
59. Look for treasure at a yard sale.
60. Try out for a play. Attend a play.
61. Collect recycling, drop it off at a recycling center or leave to be collected.
62. Play charades.
63. Have a cup of coffee and a conversation.
64. Workout.
65. Repair or refinish a piece of furniture.
66. Make a wooden flower box.
67. Wake up early in the morning and make pancakes.
68. Read a favourite poem.
69. Go dancing. Take a dance class.
70. Climb a tree.
71. Watch the sunset; watch the sunrise with a friend.

Activities for children and families

72. Design posters
73. Find out about your area's community center and/or park activities.
74. Blow bubbles.
75. Do yardwork and gardening.
76. Colour April 24-30th on a calendar and write 'National TV Turnoff Week'
77. Make a sign or banner to tape to your television stating that it's 'National TV-Turnoff Week'
78. Build a fort in the living room. Camp out for the night.
79. Research your family history and draw a family tree.

80. Invent a new game. Teach it to your friends.

81. Play an outdoor game such as hopscotch, hide and seek, or freeze-tag.

82. Organize a neighbourhood scavenger hunt.

83. Play a board game or cars with your family or friends.

84. Clean up or re-decorate your room.

85. Make puppets out of old socks. Have a puppet show.

86. Write a play at school or with friends. Perform it.

87. Construct a kite and fly it.

88. Go on a family trip.

89. In the snow, go sledding and make a snowman.

90. Create a collage out of pictures from old magazines.

91. Make a friendship bracelet and give it to a friend.

92. Draw pictures of members of your family.

93. Tell stories around a campfire.

94. Plan a slumber party.

95. Bake cookies or a cake. Invite friends over for a tea party.

96. Construct a miniature boat and float it in the water.

97. Write a letter to your grandparents. Make them a special card.

98. Ask your grandparents about what they did when they were young.

99. Make costumes using bags of old clothes and have a parade.

100. Learn about and celebrate family festivals.[2]

101. HAVE A BIG PARTY TO CELEBRATE TV-FREE WEEK!

Source: TV-Turnoff Network: www.tvturnoff.org

[1] For a beautiful and easy to use guide to stargazing with monthly sky charts for tracking the planets and stars, see the annual *Star and Planets Almanac* published by Hawthorn Press.

[2] See the following popular guides published by Hawthorn Press: *Festivals, Family and Food* by Diana Carey and Judith Large; and *Festivals Together* by Sue Fitzjohn, Minda Weston and Judith Large.

Appendix 5:
Contacts and Resources

Alliance for Childhood

Brazil
Alianca para Infancia
Luiza Lameirao e Ute Craemer,
Av. Tomas de Souza 552,
05836-350 Sao Paulo
Tel: (+55) 11 585 15370 Fax: (+55) 11 585 11089
Email: ascmazul@amcham.co.br
www.sab.org.br/monteazul

Germany
The Alliance for Childhood,
c/o International Waldorf Kindergarten Association,
D-70188 Stuttgart, Heubergstrasse 18, Germany
Email: Inter.waldorf@t-online.de

Republic of South Africa
Alliance for Childhood
Jennifer Skillen and Yvonne Herring
Greenhaus, 3 Eskol Lane, Constantia,
7800 Cape Town, RSA
Tel/Fax 0027 21 788 7867
Email: childall@skillen.wcape.school.za

Sweden
Alliance for Childhood
Dragonvagen 13, S-177675 Jarfalla
Tel/Fax: (+46) 85835 8516
E-mail: sekretariatet@waldorf.se

United Kingdom
The Alliance for Childhood, Kidbrooke Park, Forest Row,
East Sussex, RH18 5JA, UK
Email: alliance@waldorf.compulink.co.uk
www.allianceforchildhood.org.uk

United States of America
The Alliance for Childhood, PO Box 444, College Park,
MD 20741, USA
Email: jalmon@erols.com
www.allianceforchildhood.org

Fair Play for Children
35 Lyon Street, Bognor Regis, West Sussex PO 21 1BW
Tel/Fax: (+44) 01243 869922
Email: fairplay@arunet.co.uk
www.arunet.co.uk/fairplay/relate.htm

The International Association for the Child's Right to Play
Secretary: Dr Marcy Guddemi, Dept. of Education and Research,
Kindercare, 2400 President's Drive,
P.O. Box 2151, Montgomery, AL 36116 2151, USA
Tel: (+1) 334 2775090 Fax: (+1) 31104172095
Email: mguddemi@kindercare.com
www.ncsu.edu/ipa

International Save the Children Alliance
275-281 King Street, London, W6 9LZ
Tel: (+44) 020 87482554 Fax: (+44) 020 82378000
Email: info@save-children-alliance.org

Let the Children Play
Hillview, Portway Hill, Lamyatt, Shepton Mallet,
Somerset BA4 6NJ UK
Tel: (+44) 01749 813260 or 01749 813971
Email: info@letthechildrenplay.org.uk
www.letthechildrenplay.org.uk

The National Children's Bureau and Children's Play Council
8, Wakley Street, London EC1V 7QE
Tel: (+44) 020 78436000 Fax: (+44) 020 72789512
www.ncb.org.uk

National Playing Fields Association
Stanley House,, St. Chad's Place,
London WC1X 9HH
Tel: (+44) 020 78335360 Fax: (+44) 020 78335365
Email: admin@npfa.co.uk
www.npfa.co.uk (includes contact details of local, county and country branches)

Building Peace Through Play
Ruth Taronno, Coordinator
745 Westminster Ave,
Winnipeg, Manitoba R3G 1A5
Tel/Fax: (+1) 204 7758178
www.media-awareness.ca/eng/med/home/advoc/bptplay.htm

Save the Children
www.savethechildren.org

The Lion and the Lamb Project
4300 Montgomery Avenue – Suite 104
Bethesda, Maryland 20814, USA
Tel: (+1) 301 654-3091 Fax: (+1) 301 6542921
Email: lionlamb@lionlamb.org
www.lionlamb.org

The Early Years Trainers Anti Racist Network
PO Box 28
Wallasey CH45 9NP
Tel/Fax: (+44) 01516 396136

The Working Group Against Racism in Children's Resources
460 Wandsworth Road,
London SW8 3LK
Tel: (+44) 020 76274594

TV-Turnoff Network (formerly TVFree America)
1601 Connecticut Avenue, NW (303
Washington, DC 20009 USA
Tel: (+1)202 5185556 Fax: (+1)202 5185560
Email: email@tvturnoff.org
www.tvturnoff.org

Steiner Waldorf Schools Fellowship
Kidbrooke Park, Forest Row
Sussex RH18 5JA
Tel: (+44) 01342 822115 Fax: (+44) 01342 826004
Email: mail@waldorf.compulink.co.uk
www.steinerwaldorf.org.uk

Useful Web Sites

'Marketing to Children'
www.jbcc.harvard.edu/media/marketing_to_children.htm

'Children and Television Violence'
www.abelard.org/tv/tv.htm

'How TV Affects Your Child'
www.kidshealth.org/parent/positive/family/tv_affects_child_prt.htm

Other books from Hawthorn Press

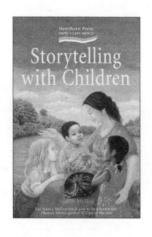

Storytelling with Children
Nancy Mellon

Telling stories awakens wonder and creates special occasions with children, whether it is bedtime, around the fire or on rainy days. Nancy Mellon shows how you can become a confident storyteller and enrich your family with the power of story.

192pp; 216 x 138mm; illustrations; paperback; 1 903458 08 0

Free Range Education
How home education works
Terri Dowty (ed)

Welcome to this essential handbook for families considering or starting out in home education. *Free Range Education* is full of family stories, resources, burning questions, humour, tips, practical steps and useful advice so you can choose what best suits your family situation. You are already your child's main teacher and these families show how home education can work for you. Both parents and children offer useful guidance, based on their experience.

256pp; 210 x 148mm; cartoons; paperback; 1 903458 07 2

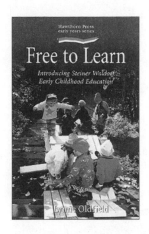

Free to Learn
Introducing Steiner Waldorf early childhood education
Lynne Oldfield

Free to Learn is a unique guide to the prin-ciples and methods of Steiner Waldorf early childhood education. This authoritative introduction is written by Lynne Oldfield, Director of the London Steiner Waldorf Early Childhood Teacher Training course. She draws on kindergarten experience from around the world, with stories, helpful insights, lively observations and pictures. This inspiring book will interest parents, educators and early years students. It is up to date, comprehensive, includes many photos and has a 16 page colour section.

256pp; 216 x 138mm; photographs; paperback; 1 903458 06 4

Helping Children to Overcome Fear
The healing power of play
Russell Evans

Critical illness can cause overwhelming feelings of abandonment and loss. Difficult for adults to face alone, for children the experience is magnified. Jean Evans was a play leader who recognised ahead of her time the importance of enabling children to give voice to their feelings, providing opportunities for play and working in partnership with parents.

128pp; 216 x 138mm
paperback
1 903458 02 1

Games Children Play
How games and sport help children develop
Kim Brooking-Payne
Illustrated by Marije Rowling

Games Children Play offers an accessible guide to games with children of age 3 upwards. These games are all tried and tested, and are the basis for the author's extensive teacher training work. The book explores children's personal development and how this is expressed in movement, play, songs and games. Each game is clearly and simply described, with diagrams or drawings, and accompanied by an explanation of why this game is helpful at a particular age. The equipment that may be needed is basic, cheap and easily available.

192pp; 297 x 210mm; paperback; 1 869 890 78 7

Muddles, Puddles and Sunshine
Your activity book to help when someone has died
Winston's Wish

Muddles, Puddles and Sunshine offers practical and sensitive support for bereaved children. Beautifully illustrated in colour, it suggests a helpful series of activities and

exercises accompanied by the friendly characters of Bee and Bear.

32pp; 297 x 210mm landscape; illustrations; paperback; 1 869 890 58 2

Pull the Other One!
String Games and Stories Book 1
Michael Taylor

This well-travelled and entertaining series of tales is accompanied by clear instructions and explanatory diagrams – guaranteed not to tie you in knots and will teach you tricks with which to dazzle your friends! With something for everyone, these ingenious tricks and tales are developed and taught with utter simplicity, making them suitable from age 5 upwards.

128pp; 216 x 148mm; drawings; paperback; 1 869 890 49 3

Kinder Dolls
A Waldorf doll-making handbook
Maricristin Sealey

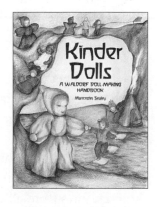

Kinder Dolls shows how to create hand-crafted dolls from natural materials. A range of simple, colourful designs will inspire both beginners and experienced doll makers alike. These dolls are old favourites, originating in Waldorf Steiner kindergartens where parents make dolls together for their children, and for the school.

'Maricristin's book is a fine source for the beginner doll maker. It is a valuable primer, full of practical tips, simple designs and clear, easy to follow instructions.'

Sara McDonald, Magic Cabin Dolls

160pp; 246 x 189mm; drawings; paperback; 1 903458 03 X

All Year Round
Ann Druitt, Christine Fynes-Clinton,
Marije Rowling

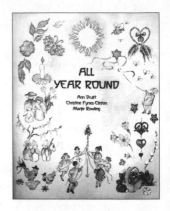

All Year Round is brimming with things
to make; activities, stories, poems and
songs to share with your family. It is
full of well illustrated ideas for fun
and celebration: from Candlemas to
Christmas and Midsummer's day to
the Winter solstice. Observing the
round of festivals is an enjoyable way to bring rhythm into
children's lives and provide a series of meaningful landmarks to
look forward to. Each festival has a special character of its own:
participation can deepen our understanding and love of nature
and bring a gift to the whole family.

320pp; 250 x 200mm; drawings; paperback; 1 869 890 47 7

Festivals Together
A guide to multicultural celebration
Sue Fitzjohn, Minda Weston, Judy Large

This special book for families and
teachers helps you celebrate festivals
from cultures from all over the world.
This resource guide for celebration
introduces a selection of 26 Buddhist,
Christian, Hindu, Jewish, Muslim and
Sikh festivals. It offers a lively intro-
duction to the wealth of different ways of life. There are stories,
things to make, recipes, songs, customs and activities for each
festival, comprehensively illustrated.

224pp; 250 x 200mm; illustrations; paperback; 1 869 890 46 9

Festivals, Family and Food
Diana Carey and Judy Large

A source of stories, recipes, things to make, activities, poems, songs and festivals. Each festival such as Christmas, Candlemas and Martinmas has its own, well illustrated chapter. There are also sections on Birthdays, Rainy Days, Convalescence and a birthday Calendar. The perfect present for a family, it explores the numerous festivals that children love celebrating.

224pp; 250 x 200mm illustrations; paperback
0 950 706 23 X

The Children's Year
Crafts and clothes for children and parents to make
Stephanie Cooper, Christine Fynes-Clinton, Marije Rowling

You needn't be an experienced craftsperson to create beautiful things! This step by step, well illustrated book with clear instructions shows you how to get started. Children and parents are encouraged to try all sorts of handwork, with different projects relating to the seasons of the year. Here are soft toys, wooden toys, moving toys such as balancing birds or climbing gnomes,

horses, woolly hats, mobiles and dolls. There are over 100 treasures to make in seasonal groupings around the children's year.

192pp; 250 x 200mm; drawings; paperback; 1 869 890 00 0

Getting in touch with Hawthorn Press

What are your pressing questions about the early years?
The Hawthorn Early Years Series arises from parents' and educators' pressing questions and concerns – so please contact us with your questions. These will help spark new books, workshops or festivals if there is sufficient interest. We will be delighted to hear your views on our Early Years books, how they can be improved, and what your needs are.

Visit our website for details of the Early Years Series and forthcoming books and events:

http://www.hawthornpress.com

Ordering books

If you have difficulties ordering Hawthorn Press books from a bookshop, you can order direct from:

United Kingdom
Scottish Book Source Distribution,
137 Dundee Street, Edinburgh,
EH11 1BG
Tel: 0131 229 6800 Fax: 0131 229 9070

North America
Anthroposophic Press c/o Books International,
PO Box 960,
Herndon, VA 201 72-0960.
Toll free order line: 800-856-8664
Toll free fax line: 800-277-9747

Dear Reader

If you wish to follow up your reading of this book, please tick the boxes below as appropriate, fill in your name and address and return to Hawthorn Press:

☐   Please send me a catalogue of other Hawthorn Press books.

☐   Please send me details of Early Years events and courses.

Questions I have about the Early Years are:

_____

_____

_____

_____

_____

Name   _____

Address   _____

_____

_____

Postcode _____ Tel. no. _____

Please return to: Hawthorn Press, Hawthorn House,
1 Lansdown Lane, Stroud, Glos. GL5 1BJ, UK
or Fax (01453) 751138